Series/Number 07-129

D0168374

EFFECT SIZE FOR ANOVA DESIGNS

JOSE M. CORTINA
George Mason University

HOSSEIN NOURI
College of New Jersey

SAGE PUBLICATIONS
International Educational and Professional Publisher
Thousand Oaks   London   New Delhi

For information:

SAGE Publications, Inc.
2455 Teller Road
Thousand Oaks, California 91320
E-mail: order@sagepub.com

SAGE Publications Ltd.
6 Bonhill Street
London EC2A 4PU
United Kingdom

SAGE Publications India Pvt. Ltd.
M-32 Market
Greater Kailash I
New Delhi 110 048 India

Printed in the United States of America

Library of Congress Cataloging-in-Publication Data

Cortina, Jose M.
    Effect size for ANOVA designs / by Jose M. Cortina and Hossein Nouri.
    p. cm. — (Sage university papers series. Quantitative applications in the social sciences; 07-129)
    Includes bibliographical references.
    ISBN 0-7619-1550-8 (acid-free paper)
    1. Experimental design. 2. Analysis of variance. I. Nouri, Hossein. II. Title. III. Series: Sage university papers series. Quantitative applications in the social sciences ; no. 07-129.
    QA279 .C6645   1999
    519.5'38—dc21   99-6532

05 06 7 6 5 4

When citing a university paper, please use the proper form. Remember to cite the Sage University Paper series title and include the paper number. One of the following formats can be adapted (depending on the style manual used):

(1) CORTINA, JOSE M. (2000) Effect size for ANOVA designs. Sage University Papers Series on Quantitative Applications in the Social Sciences, 07-129. Thousand Oaks, CA: Sage.

OR

(2) Cortina, J. M. (2000). *Effect size for ANOVA designs*. (Sage University Papers Series on Quantitative Applications in the Social Sciences, series no. 07-129). Thousand Oaks, CA: Sage.

ω

CONTENTS

SERIES EDITOR'S INTRODUCTION

How big is the effect of an independent variable? That may well be the principal question a researcher asks, at least once it is established that the effect is significantly different from zero. Even with the simplest of designs, however, it may not be easy to assess the magnitude of an effect. Suppose an education psychologist is assessing reading speed in a two independent group study, where there are 50 randomly assigned college sophomores in each. Group A reads a guide to improving reading speed, whereas Group B receives a lecture on speed reading. After exposure to these treatments, subjects take a multitude item test measuring comprehended words (CW). For Group A the mean CW = 54.6, and for Group B the mean CW = 65.1. The difference of 11.5 is found to be statistically significant at .05, suggesting that the lecture improved reading speed. But how big is that effect? Is 11.5 a "big number?" We cannot say unless we know more. In particular, we need to know the spread of scores of the reading speed variable. On the one hand, if in the population CW is normally distributed and goes from 2.1 to 306.7, then the effect—11.5—covers only a little part of the range and must appear small. On the other hand, if that range is from 2.1 to 30.6, then the effect appears large.

One approach to this variability problem is standardization of the effect measure. The authors emphasize the use of "d," which essentially divides the observed effect by the standard deviation of the dependent variable. In our example, we would divide the mean difference (11.5) by the pooled standard deviation of CW (28.3), yielding $d = .41$. This suggests that the effects of the instructional change is moderate, a conclusion reinforced by the conversion of d to a Pearson's r of .20. (The general conversion formula is provided therein).

Calculating d can become complicated with more complex designs. Fortunately, in this single source Dr. Cortina and Dr. Nouri carefully layout the computational methods for d with a variety of designs, including factorial ANOVA, ANCOVA, and repeated measures ANOVA. Also, they develop rules for the "second-hand" calculations needed to arrive at d values from other studies, necessary in order to carry out meta-analyses. Throughout, the computations are illustrated on the same data, a comprehensive set of simulated observations on air traffic controllers. The dependent variable is always a task performance, related to different independent variables, and showing effect size calculation under the different ANOVA designs. While the text throughly covers computational steps, it goes beyond them to raise important theoretical issues. An innovative discussion of the place of "off-factors," in arriving at effect size, is given. Also, in the closing chapter, important questions of research practice are raised. How different are the different measures of d? What about changing variance in the independent variables? In a meta-analysis, should one rely on d or r? Is unequal subgroup size a problem? Should research reporting guidelines be altered? These are all issues that the "thinking practioner" must weigh when actually writing up and interpreting his or her own results, from an assessment of effect size based on the computational methods in this excellent handbook.

—*Michael S. Lewis-Beck*
Series Editor

EFFECT SIZE FOR ANOVA DESIGNS

JOSE M. CORTINA
George Mason University

HOSSEIN NOURI
The College of New Jersey

INTRODUCTION

There was a time, not long ago, when we social scientists relied almost entirely on tests of statistical significance to provide us with the information that we needed to draw our conclusions. The significance test is not without its advantages (Cortina & Dunlap, 1997), but it also suffers from certain limitations. The limitation of primary interest here is that tests of statistical significance are affected greatly by sample size. Thus, for example, a very weak effect can be "statistically significant" while a fairly strong effect can fail to attain statistical significance (see Meehl, 1990 for examples of the former, and Hunter & Schmidt, 1990 for examples of the latter).

Due to these interpretational limitations, we often want information relating not only to the question of whether or not an effect exists, but also to the magnitude of the effect. This is typically accomplished by standardizing some index of raw magnitude (e.g., a difference between group means) so that variability is held constant across variables or studies. The result is an index such as d, r^2, or η^2.

For many research designs, the computation of standardized magnitude indices is quite simple. For example, if we employ a two-group design, we can compute d by finding the difference between the group means and dividing by the pooled or control group standard deviation. Moreover, this value gives us an index of magnitude of effect for both the independent groups and repeated measures designs. If instead we employ a simple correlational design with continuous variables, then the Pearson correlation coefficient provides an analogous index. Of course, the point-biserial correlation coefficient, d, $F_{1, N1+N2-2}$, and $t_{N1+N2-2}$ are easily converted into one another

1

with readily available formulas (see our Table 2.1 or Hunter & Schmidt, 1990, p. 273).[1] For more complicated designs, computation of standardized magnitude indices is not necessarily so simple. If, for example, we were to take the two-group design and add a covariate such that we wanted an index of magnitude of effect with the covariate held constant, computation is, as we see later in this monograph, no longer straightforward. These more complicated designs also make second-hand computation of magnitude indices more difficult. By second-hand, we mean computations, typical of meta-analysis, that must be performed on results as reported in written work. Suppose that we are conducting a meta-analysis of the relationship between mental practice and task performance. Some of the studies from which we would like to extract information might have employed two-group, repeated measures designs such that task performance was measured for each participant after mental practice and after no practice. If these studies reported group means and standard deviations, then d values are easily calculated using the formula described above. Oftentimes, however, effect size values must be computed from test statistics such as t values. In order to convert a repeated measures t value into a d value, we must rely on the authors of these studies to provide us with descriptive information such as the measure to measure correlations. We must also know how to use this information to generate the values that we need.

As researchers often find themselves facing such complex designs, there exists a need for clarification regarding the methods that might be used to compute effect size values from such designs. To this end, the purpose of this monograph is to describe methods for computing indices of standardized magnitude of effect from complex ANOVA designs. By "complex" we simply mean designs that involve repeated measurements, multiple independent variables, or covariates. Thus, we focus on repeated measures ANOVA, factorial ANOVA, and ANCOVA designs. MANOVA, MANCOVA, and correlational designs are beyond the scope of this manuscript.

As is true of most or all of the QASS monographs, much (though not all) of the material in the present monograph has been presented before, if not by one of the present authors, then by others. It is our hope that this monograph can serve as a single resource that accommodates a variety of needs viz. effect size computation for ANOVA designs and that does so in a way that makes the procedures as accessible to researchers as possible.

It should be noted that some of the procedures described below are relevant only for the second-hand computations common in meta-analysis. For example, the procedures in Chapter 3 attributed to Morris and DeShon (1997) and Glass, McGaw, and Smith (1981) are most useful when cell means from an ANOVA are not available, and effect size values must be computed from other information typically contained in published reports. Other procedures, such as the Nouri and Greenberg (1995) procedure, are relevant for situations in which one has access to relevant summary statistics (i.e., means and standard deviations) or to primary data.

The Data Set

A single data set is used to demonstrate the techniques to be described. The full data set is contained in Appendix A. It can also be downloaded from the web at www.gmu.edu/departments/psychology/homepage/cortina. These data were simulated to represent the results of an attempt to predict performance on an air traffic controller (ATC) task. The dependent variable is performance on the task. The independent group variables–covariates are conscientiousness, field independence, sex, exposure to a training video, race, intelligence, amount of caffeine consumed, and type of screen display. The repeated measures independent variables are number of targets present on the screen and speed of targets. Our intention in generating this data set was to provide opportunities to demonstrate computations for all relevant designs while keeping the example realistic and the number of variables at a manageable level. Thus, we have two continuous variables that can serve as covariates (intelligence, conscientiousness), three dichotomous independent groups variables (high–low-field independence, gender, exposure to a training video), three trichotomous independent groups variables (race, caffeine, type of screen display), and two trichotomous repeated measures variables (number of targets, target speed). The only remaining variable is labeled JOBPERF and is intended to represent an additional measurement on the dependent variable apart from those associated with the repeated measures variables. This variable will be used for any purely independent groups design illustrations.

4

The monograph unfolds as follows. We begin in Chapter 1 with a review of effect size computation for simple, independent group designs with two groups. This should give us some firm conceptual and computational footing as we move on to the more complicated areas. In Chapter 2, we show how the situation changes if the independent variable contains more than two groups. Chapter 3 contains descriptions of procedures for computing effect size values in factorial independent groups designs. In Chapter 4, we add covariates to the mix and show how the computations change. Chapter 5 deals with various repeated measures designs. The final chapter of the monograph contains discussions of ancillary issues such as standardized versus unstandardized indices of effect magnitude and inferences from fixed versus random effects designs.

Before moving on, we offer one final suggestion. This monograph, like many in this series, contains its fair share of equations. Some are harder on the eye than others, but all of them are easier to use than it may at first seem. Before the eyes start to glaze over, we suggest the reader look more carefully at the components of the equations and the examples that are given. We feel confident that even the most harrowing of these equations prove to be manageable for the average reader.

1. THE TWO INDEPENDENT GROUP DESIGN: A REVIEW[2]

In this simple design, one group of people is exposed to or possesses one level of a dichotomous variable, while a different group of people is exposed to or possesses the other level of the variable. Of ultimate interest is the difference in the dependent variable scores between the two groups.

Example 1.1. Suppose we are interested in differences in performance on the air traffic controller task described in Appendix A between people who are high in field independence and people who are low in field independence. The relevant values are reported in Table 1.1.

Mean performance on the task for the 150 "high-field independence" people included in the sample was 9.03, while mean perfor-

TABLE 1.1

Two Independent Groups

	N	Mean	Std. dev.	Variance
High-field independence	150	9.03	1.96	3.84
Low-field independence	150	7.46	2.13	4.53

$s_p = \text{SQRT}\{[(N_1 - 1)s_1^2 + (N_2 - 1)s_2^2]/[N_1 + N_2 - 2]\}$
$\quad = [(149*3.84) + (149*4.53)]/298 = 2.04$
$d = (9.03 - 7.46)/2.04 = .77$
$r = .36$
$t = 6.66$
$\sigma_e^2 = [N - 1/N - 3][(4/N)(1 + \delta^2/8)] = (299/297)(4/300)(1 + .77^2/8) = .0144$

mance on the task for the 150 "low-field independence" people was 7.46. Thus, the difference in means was 1.57. In the absence of other information, this difference value is difficult to interpret. If there is a tremendous amount of variability in the dependent variable, then 1.57 might represent a fairly small difference. If, on the other hand, scores only ranged from 5 to 11, then 1.57 is a considerable difference. A further interpretational difficulty enters the picture if we wish to compare this finding with a comparable finding from another study. Suppose the dependent variable score for a person in our study was the number of targets for which a correct decision was made over the course of an hour, whereas in another study, correct decisions were counted over 3 hours. In this case, the second study might yield a larger mean difference value than our study even if the phenomenon being studied is the same (see Cortina & DeShon, 1998 for a more detailed discussion of the advantages of standardized indices).

The solution is, of course, to take variabilities within the studies into account. Thus, in each study, we would divide the mean difference by an estimate of the standard deviation of individual scores in the population. The value that represents this estimate is typically either the control group standard deviation or the pooled standard deviation (Cohen, 1969). In the present case, there is no obvious control group, so we might use the pooled standard deviation instead, where

$$s_p = \left\{[(N_1 - 1)s_1^2 + (N_2 - 1)s_2^2]/[N_1 + N_2 - 2]\right\}^{.5} \quad (1.1)$$

where the Ns and s^2s are within group sample sizes and variances, respectively.
Thus, d becomes

$$(\bar{x}_1 - \bar{x}_2)/s_p \qquad (1.2)$$

where $\bar{x}_i$ is the mean for group i.

It should be noted that Hedges (1981) showed that under the homogeneity of variance assumption, the effect size estimator based on the control group standard deviation is biased and that a better estimator results when the control group standard deviation is replaced with the pooled standard deviation (s_p). Hunter and Schmidt (1990) note two advantages to using the pooled within group standard deviation (s_p) rather than the control group standard deviation (s_C). First, s_C has a larger sampling error than does s_p. Second, some studies report a value for t or F which can be transformed to d as estimated using s_p. These studies may not report within group standard deviations, which in turn makes computation of effect size using the s_C impossible. In this monograph, we use Equation (1.1) for estimating the denominator of the effect size formula, s_p.

It should also be noted that circumstances sometimes exist in which it may be useful to replace the pooled standard deviation with an error term that takes into account the effects of other independent variables. One could argue that such an index should not be labeled an "effect size," but we will leave the semantic quibbling to others. In any case, this topic is revisited in Chapter 3. For these first two chapters, we focus only on the ordinary pooled standard deviation as a denominator for the effect size index.

Now, back to the example. For our data, Equation (1.1) yields a value of 2.04. If we divide the mean difference value by this pooled standard deviation, we get the d statistic, 0.77. Similar operations for the values from other studies would give values that can be directly compared to this one because d is simply the mean difference if the dependent variable were scaled to have unit variance within groups (Hedges & Olkin, 1985). Also, because d and r are algebraic transformations of one another, d is easily interpreted. The conversion formulas are

$$r = d/(4 + d^2)^{.5}, \qquad (1.3)$$

and

$$d = 2r/(1 - r^2)^{.5}. \tag{1.4}$$

Thus, the point-biserial correlation (a special case of Pearson's r) between our field independence variable and task performance is estimated[3] to be .36 (see Hunter & Schmidt, 1990, Chap. 7 for detailed discussions of these formulas).

The d value can be interpreted in several equivalent ways. It can be interpreted in terms of the overlap between the two population distributions in question (Cohen, 1969). For a d value of 0.77, Cohen's tables show that approximately 46% of the area covered by the two distributions combined is unique to one or the other distribution. This also means that the performance of people at the 50% percentile of the high-field independence population exceeds that of approximately 78% of the low-field independence population. Said another way, d represents the proportion of control group scores that are less than the average score in the experimental group, assuming a beneficial treatment and normal distributions (Hedges & Olkin, 1985).

Thus, owing in large part to its standardized nature, the d value can be very useful for purposes of interpretation. In the context of meta-analysis, it is important to note that many published pieces do not contain all of the summary statistics necessary to compute these effect size values. In the simple two independent group case, this does not pose much of a problem, as d is easily calculated from test statistics as well as from summary statistics. Specifically,

$$d = t[(1/n_1) + (1/n_2)]^{.5}, \tag{1.5}$$

where the ns are the within group sample sizes.[4] In the present example involving field independence, $t = 6.66$. Equation (1.5) can be used to convert this into $d = .77$, just as before.

So, computation of effect size values from studies involving two independent groups is simple enough as long as either the appropriate summary or test statistics are available. Such information is always available at the primary study level and is usually available for cumulation of findings across studies. Effect size can also be approximated using information typically reported from ANOVAs. The resulting value is a standardized index of magnitude of effect and can be used to compare the contributions of different variables within a given study or the contributions of the same variable across different studies.

Estimation of Sampling Error Variance

It is often useful to estimate not only the effect size value, but also the variance or standard deviation of the effect size estimate (i.e., the standard error). In particular, sampling error variance estimates are necessary for formation of confidence intervals and for computation of various meta-analytic statistics.

Hunter and Schmidt (1990) offer the following formula for the variance of d (denoted σ_e^2 where e is for sampling error)

$$\sigma_e^2 = [(N - 1)/(N - 3)][(4/N)(1 + \delta^2/8)], \qquad (1.6)$$

where N is the total sample size and δ is the population effect size, estimated with d. With reasonable sample sizes, the ratio of degrees of freedom in the left-hand portion of the formula can be dropped without any great loss. For the example above, $d = .77$, $N = 300$, and sampling error variance therefore equals

$$\sigma_e^2 = [299/297][(4/300)(1 + .77^2/8)] = .0144.$$

The standard error of d would be $.0144^{.5} = .12$. This value could then be used to form confidence intervals around the effect size estimate using the formula

$$CI_\alpha = (d - C_{\alpha/2} * \sigma_e) \le \delta \le (d + C_{\alpha/2} * \sigma_e), \qquad (1.7)$$

where d is the effect size estimate, $C_{\alpha/2}$ is the appropriate two-tailed value for the standard normal distribution (e.g., 1.96 for the 95% interval), and σ_e is the standard error of the d statistic, computed from Equation (1.6).

For the present example, the 95% confidence interval would be

$$.77 - 1.96 * \sigma_e \leq \delta \leq .77 + 1.96 * \sigma_e = .535 \leq \delta \leq 1.01.$$

Thus, we can be 95% certain that the population effect size δ is between .53 and 1.01. Moreover, because this interval does not contain 0, we would reject the null hypothesis $\delta = 0$ with a two-tailed test and a significance level of .05. Indeed, we would reject the null hypothesis $\delta = .5$ with such a test.

Because the procedures that we describe in this monograph yield d values, the procedures for computing sampling error variances are typically the same across procedures. Where this is not the case, we attempt to describe alternative formulas for producing sampling error variance values.

Before moving on, one final issue must be discussed. There exists a lack of consistency regarding the symbols used to represent effect size based on mean differences. Glass et al. (1981) use d to denote the mean difference divided by the *control group* standard deviation. Cohen (1969) and Hunter and Schmidt (1990) use d to denote mean difference divided by the pooled standard deviation computed using our Equation (1.1). Hedges and Olkin (1985) use "g" instead of d to denote this value. These authors note that there is a small sample bias in Equation (1.2) and use d to denote their unbiased estimator (denoted d^* by Hunter & Schmidt, 1990):

$$d = g\{1 - [3/(4N - 9)]\}. \tag{1.8}$$

Of course, the values yielded by Equations (1.2) and (1.8) will be very similar for all but very small samples. If we use Equation (1.8) to compute a d value for Example 1.1, we arrive at the same result within rounding error, .77.

Hedges (1981) gives the formula for the variance of this estimator as

$$\sigma_d^2 = [(n_E + n_C)/(n_E n_C)] + \{d^2/[2(n_E + n_C)]\}. \tag{1.9}$$

For Example 1.1, this equation yields a value of .0143, which compares favorably with the value from Equation (1.6), .0144.

Others, such as Morris and DeShon (1997) also use g to denote the value yielded by our Equation (1.2). For the present monograph, we use d to denote Cohen's d, which is given in our Equation (1.2). Its sampling error variance is given by our Equation (1.6).

Summary

In this chapter, we demonstrated the usefulness of standardized indices of effect magnitude. This was followed by descriptions of the two independent group design and the methods available for computing effect size values therefrom using both summary and test statistics. Finally, we pointed out the different uses of d in the literature and defined the term as it is used in the remainder of this monograph.

2. ONE-WAY INDEPENDENT GROUPS DESIGNS

Extracting relevant information from a one-way independent groups design with more than two levels is (or at least can be) more complicated. The handling of the data from such designs depends first on whether or not the $k > 2$ levels are ordered. If they are ordered, then a standard effect size value such as η^2 or ω^2 can be computed. Unlike Pearson's r, each of these statistics is nondirectional and takes into account both linear and curvilinear effects. The formulas for these values are

$$\eta^2 = (SS_{\text{total}} - SS_{\text{error}})/SS_{\text{total}}, \qquad (2.1)$$

and

$$\omega^2 = (SS_{\text{treatment}} - (k - 1)MS_{\text{error}})/(SS_{\text{total}} + MS_{\text{error}}). \quad (2.2)$$

It should be noted that ω^2, while more complicated, is less biased than η^2. Also worth noting is the fact that many researchers believe that the proper indices of relationships involving ordinal variables are polyserial and polychoric correlations (e.g., Joreskog & Sorbom, 1996). These values are computed based not only on the observed data, but also on assumptions regarding the underlying distributions of the variables involved. While it is possible to compute such values from raw data, it is typically impossible to do so from values reported in the typical research report. Thus, use of such values may be impractical for meta-analytic applications.

If the levels of the independent variable are not ordered, then our interest is typically in only two (or in pairs) of the included levels. Consider the goal-setting example presented on p. 804 of Nouri and Greenberg (1995). The independent variable of interest was type of goal, and the dependent variable was job performance. The goal variable had three levels: participative, assigned, and "do your best." Obviously, this three-level variable has little meaning unless it is broken down into its parts. Thus, we might want to know how people who have set goals participatively perform relative to people to whom goals have been assigned. Alternatively, we might want to know if performance is higher for people to whom a goal has been assigned relative to people told to do their best. In either case, the comparisons involve only two of the available levels.

If one-way ANOVA is used to compare *two* groups, the estimation of the effect size involves operations similar to those discussed in Chapter 1. That is, we can convert $F_{1, N1 + N2 - 2}$ to d as shown in Table 2.1. When more than two groups are involved, summary statistics must be used to compute the relevant mean and pooled standard deviation values.

If neither $F_{1, N1 + N2 - 2}$ (or $t_{N1 + N2 - 2}$, which equals the square root of F for the two-group case) nor within group standard deviations are available, d can be approximated using the following formula for

TABLE 2.1
Conversions Formulas for the Two-Group Design

Information Given	Estimation Formula	Comments
$t_{DF_{error}}$	$d = t[(1/n_E) + (1/n_C)]^{.5}$	For unequal groups
	$d = 2t/(DF_{within})^{.5}$ or $d = t(2/n_C)^{.5}$	For reasonably equal groups
$F_{1, DF_{error}}$	$d = (F)^{.5}[(1/n_E) + (1/n_C)]^{.5}$	For unequal groups
	$d = 2[F/(DF_{within})]^{.5}$	For reasonably equal groups
Z test	$d = 2Z/(N)^{.5}$	$N = n_E + n_C$
r	$d = [r/(1 - r^2)^{.5}][df(n_E + n_C)/n_E n_C]^{.5}$	

12

pooled standard deviation offered by Ray and Shadish (1996):

$$S = \left\{ \left[\sum_{i=1}^{K} n_i (\bar{x}_i - G)^2 / (k - 1) \right] \Big/ F \right\}^{.5}, \qquad (2.3)$$

where n_i is the sample size for the ith group, $\bar{x}_i$ is the mean of the ith group, $G = \Sigma n_i \bar{x}_i$, k is the number of groups, and F is the overall F ratio. Alternatively, the pooled standard deviation can be estimated as $(MS_{within})^{.5}$.

Example 2.1. In this example, we use the JOBPERF variable from Table 1.1 as the dependent variable and the trichotomous display type variable (labeled "DISPCAT1") as the independent variable. The three values for this independent variable are $0 =$ "display screen is updated every 10 s," $1 =$ "display screen is updated every 5 s," and $2 =$ "display screen is updated continuously." Table 2.2 presents relevant summary statistics and one-way ANOVA results.

Suppose that our interest is in the increase in performance on the ATC task that might be associated with a change from the 10 s updated display to the 5 s update display. If within group means, standard deviations, and sample sizes are available, as they would be for any primary study, then d can be computed directly using

TABLE 2.2
One-way ANOVA

Display Category	N	Mean	Std. Dev	Variance
10 s update	102	8.02	2.26	5.11
5 s update	99	8.48	2.28	5.21
Continuous display	99	8.24	1.99	3.97
$t_{10 \text{ s versus } 5 \text{ s}} = 1.44$				

	ANOVA Summary Table			
Source	df	SS	MS	F
Between groups	2	10.72	5.36	1.12
Within groups	297	1417.97	4.77	
Total	299	1428.7		

Equation (1.2):

$$(\bar{x}_1 - \bar{x}_2)/s_p,$$

$$d = (8.48 - 8.02)/s_p,$$

$$s_p = \left\{\left[(N_1 - 1)s_1^2 + (N_2 - 1)s_2^2\right]/\left[N_1 + N_2 - 2\right]\right\}^{.5},$$

$$s_p = \left\{\left[(101*5.11) + (98*5.2)\right]/198\right\}^{.5} = 2.27,$$

$$d = .46/2.27 = .203.$$

If a post hoc t test comparing the means of interest were available, then d could be computed using Equation (1.5). Then

$$d = 1.44[(1/102) + (1/99)]^{.5} = .203.$$

If group means, sample sizes, and an overall F value were available, then the pooled standard deviation could be approximated with Equation (2.3),

$$s_p = \left\{\left\{\left[102*(8.02 - 8.24)^2\right] + \left[99*(8.48 - 8.24)^2\right]\right.\right.$$

$$\left.\left. + \left[99*(8.24 - 8.24)^2\right]/2\right\}/1.12\right\}^{.5} = 2.18,$$

yielding

$$d = .46/2.18 = .211.$$

Finally, the square root of the mean squares within groups from the ANOVA could be used to approximate the pooled standard deviation, thus yielding

$$s_p = (MS_{within})^{.5} = 4.77^{.5} = 2.18,$$

$$d = .46/2.18 = .211.$$

As can be seen, these last two computations yielded values that are different from the actual effect size as computed using Equations (1.1) and (1.2). Ray and Shadish (1996, p. 1318) also note this

14

discrepancy but argue that this "pooled standard deviation is a weighted average of three or more groups compared to a weighted average of two groups in d. In randomized experiments where groups have the same variances on expectation, the two methods should yield the same standard deviations on expectation." Therefore, the use of this pooled standard deviation in circumstances where the standard deviation of groups may be relatively equal could be warranted.

Summary

This chapter dealt with effect size computation for one-way, independent group ANOVA designs. It was first pointed out that if the levels of the independent variable are ordered, then the variable can be treated essentially as a continuous variable, and statistics such as η^2 and ω^2 can be computed and used as estimates of effect size. In those situations where the levels are not ordered, then our interest, viz. effect sizes, usually lies with two of the levels. Effect size computations can then be based on certain ANOVA summary results as well as the summary and test statistics described in Chapter 1.

3. FACTORIAL INDEPENDENT GROUP DESIGNS

2 × 2 Analysis of Variance (ANOVA)

We start this chapter with a 2 × 2 factorial design and extend it to more complex factorial designs. Consider Figure 3.1.

This figure is meant to represent a situation in which subjects are randomly assigned to the experimental or control conditions under both factor A and factor B creating four independent groups. Under this design, the researcher may be interested in one or both of the main effects as well as the interaction. Although procedures are not well developed for computation of d values for interactions, procedures do exist for computation of values associated with the main effects.

Computing d values from such designs is less than straightforward even if summary statistics are available. The reason is that a given

F
A
C
T
O
R

B

	Factor A	
	Control Condition	Experimental Condition
Control condition	A	B
Experimental condition	C	D

Figure 3.1. 2 × 2 factorial.

effect must be disentangled from the other effects represented in the output. In order to understand this problem of entanglement, one must first consider the role played by the off-factors in the model.[5]

The Role of the Off-Factors

Let us return to Figure 3.1. Suppose that we are interested in computing an effect size value for factor A. Factor B would then be the off-factor for our purposes. The procedure that we use to compute an effect size value for factor A depends on the role played by factor B. If factor B varies naturally in the population to which we want to generalize, then the error term that we use to compute effect size for factor A must contain not only unexplained variance, but also variance explained by factor B. Glass et al. (1981) refer to such a variable as being of "theoretical interest." Although factor B may or may not be of actual theoretical interest, it may be necessary for testing hypotheses about factor A. Variables such as gender and race, which vary in most populations to which we might want to generalize, would be examples of such factors.

If, instead, factor B is a variable that has been inserted into the situation by the experimenter, then its influence must be removed from the error term that we use to compute effect size for factor A. Glass et al. (1981) refer to such variables as being "not of theoretical interest."

Let us give some labels to factors A and B. Suppose that factor A is the training video variable from the ATC data, and factor B is the gender variable. A two-way, independent groups, factorial ANOVA is conducted and the relevant statistics produced. Suppose further that we wish to compute an effect size value for the training video variable. This situation is not so simple as that described in the previous chapter because of the presence of both the independent variable for which we wish to compute an effect size value and the other independent variable. For purposes of standardization, *we want our effect size value to represent the d value that we would have obtained from a one-way ANOVA containing only the training video variable.* The numerator of the *d* formula is simple enough to compute as we see shortly. The trick lies in identifying the correct error value. The term effect size typically implies an estimate of population standard deviation as a denominator, but the presence of the second, off-factor complicates this estimation.

One might suggest that the square root of the MS_{within} be used because MS_{within} represents the unexplained variance. The problem with this suggestion is that the MS_{within} is the variance in the dependent variable, task peformance in the case of the present example, that remains after *removing* that associated with all of the independent variables contained in the study. This would include removal of the variance associated with gender, which is a "variable of theoretical interest," to use Glass' term. It can be expected to vary and explain variance in the *population* to which we want to generalize. Thus, the error variance from a one-way ANOVA containing only the training video variable would (and should) contain variance attributable to gender. Because the MS_{within} from the two-way ANOVA does not contain this variance attributable to gender, its square root underestimates the population standard deviation. It is only when we put the variability attributable to gender back into the MS_{within} that we obtain a reasonable estimate of the error term that would have resulted from a one-way ANOVA. This variance replacement is exactly what is done with the Nouri and Greenberg (1995), Glass et al. (1981), and Morris and DeShon (1997) procedures described below.

Now let us modify the example. Instead of using gender as the off-factor, let us use an experimentally manipulated variable. This variable has two levels: a control in which nothing of interest happens, and an experimental in which each subject is hit on the shins with the business end of a table tennis paddle every 30 s over the duration of the task. We again conduct our two-way ANOVA and again wish to compute an effect size value for the training video variable. Note that, unlike gender, our off-factor here is unlikely to vary in the population to which we want to generalize. It is, therefore, unlikely to contribute to variability in the dependent variable in the population. On the other hand, its presence in our experiment *is* likely to create more variability in our dependent variable observations. If we had conducted a one-way ANOVA with only the training video variable, the variance in the dependent variable would not have reflected any influence of our off-factor because our off-factor does not vary normally in the population to which we wish to generalize. In our two-way design, however, the variance of our dependent variable is influenced by this off-factor. Thus, the denominator of our effect size estimator must represent error variance *with our off-factor held constant.* If the off-factor is not held constant, then we overestimate the pooled variance, and therefore underestimate effect size for our training video variable. Because the Nouri and Greenberg (1995), Glass et al. (1981), and Morris and DeShon (1997) procedures include the variance attributable to the off-factor in the denominators of their effect size estimators, they result in underestimation of effect size for the factor in question when the off-factor does not occur naturally in the population. Fortunately, the solution to this problem is actually rather simple.

This is where the square root of MS_{within} from the two-way ANOVA comes in handy. Because this MS_{within} represents the variance in the dependent variable unexplained by the factors in the two-way ANOVA, it does not contain the variability induced by the off-factor. Its square root is therefore a reasonable estimate of the pooled standard deviation that would have resulted from a one-way ANOVA and can be used as the denominator of the effect size estimator.

If the factor of interest contains more than two levels, then the numerator for the effect size may be computed using Equations (3.1) or (3.2) below. The square root of the MS_{within} can serve as the denominator provided that we assume a fixed effects model viz. the entire set of values of the independent variable for which we are computing effect size.

Thus, if the off-factor is not of theoretical interest, that is, if it is not expected to vary in the population to which one wishes to generalize, then d values can be computed directly from standard ANOVA output. If, on the other hand, the off-factor is expected to vary in the population of interest, then one of the three procedures described in the next section might be used to compute effect size. The case of multiple off-factors is treated in a later section.

Effect Size in the Presence of "Real" Off-Factors

Several procedures are available for estimating effect sizes from studies in which the off-factor is expected to vary in the population. One procedure involves descriptive statistics to estimate the effect size (Nouri & Greenberg, 1995). We refer to this procedure as the $N \& G$ procedure. The other two procedures that we discuss are attributable to Morris and DeShon ($M \& D$: 1997) and Glass et al. (*Glass*: 1981). These procedures are useful primarily for meta-analytic and other cumulative applications and rely on various information commonly contained in ANOVA summary tables. Specifically, the Glass procedure can be used when sums of squares and degrees of freedom are available for all variables, while the M & D procedure can be used when F values and degrees of freedom are available for all variables. All three of these procedures require independence of factors. Although any source of independence is sufficient, independence is essentially guaranteed if subjects are randomly assigned to the treatments of at least $k - 1$ of the k independent variables.

We begin with the N & G procedure, which is applied to within cell means and standard deviations and can be used whenever such information is available assuming that these means and standard deviations come from a fixed effect design (see below for a more detailed discussion of this assumption). Based on cell information, the following formulas should be used to calculate the mean and standard deviation for each level of the factor of interest (see Nouri & Greenberg, 1995 for the derivations of the formulas):

$$\bar{x}_{i.} = (1/n_{i.}) \sum_{j=1}^{t} n_{ij} \bar{x}_{ij.}, \tag{3.1}$$

where:

$i = 1, 2, \ldots, g,$

$j = 1, 2, \ldots, t,$

$\bar{x}_{ij}$ = mean in the cell associated with the ith level of the factor of interest and the jth level of the other factor,

$\bar{x}_{i.}$ = group mean for people who received the ith level of the factor of interest,

n_{ij} = number of observations in the cell associated with the ith level of the factor of interest and the jth level of the other factor,

and

$$n_{i.} = \sum_{j=1}^{t} n_{ij}.$$

In the special case when cell sample sizes are equal, the following formula can be used

$$\bar{x}_{i.} = \sum_{j=1}^{t} \bar{x}_{ij}/t, \qquad (3.2)$$

where:

t = number of treatments in each group.

The variance values to be plugged into Equation (1.1) are calculated as

$$\sigma_{i.}^2 = \left[\sum_{j=1}^{t} (n_{ij} - 1)\sigma_{ij}^2 + \sum_{j=1}^{t} n_{ij}(\bar{x}_{ij} - \bar{x}_{i.})^2 \right] \bigg/ (n_{i.} - 1), \qquad (3.3)$$

where:

$i = 1, 2, \ldots, g,$

$j = 1, 2, \ldots, t,$

$\sigma_{i.}^2$ = variance for the group that received the ith level of the factor of interest,

σ_{ij}^2 = variance in the cell associated with the ith level of the factor of interest and the jth level of the other factor,

$\bar{x}_{ij}$ = mean in the cell associated with the ith level of the factor of interest and the jth level of the other factor,

$\bar{x}_{i.}$ = mean of the group that received the ith level of the factor of interest,

n_{ij} = number of observations in the cell associated with the ith level of the factor of interest and the jth level of the other factor,

$$n_{i.} = \sum_{j=1}^{t} n_{ij}.$$

In the special case where cell sample sizes are equal, the following formula can be used

$$\sigma_{i.}^2 = \left[(n-1) \sum_{j=1}^{t} \sigma_{ij}^2 + n \sum_{j=1}^{t} (\bar{x}_{ij} - \bar{x}_{i.})^2 \right] \Big/ (n_{i.} - 1). \quad (3.4)$$

After computing the standard deviations using the above formulas, the pooled standard deviation is estimated using Equation (1.1). Then, the pooled standard deviation is used in Equation (1.2) to estimate the effect size.

If within group standard deviations are not available, then we must look to other information in order to compute the pooled standard deviation. Unfortunately, the Ray and Shadish (1996) formula is not a viable alternative, and neither does the square root of the MS_{within} suffice for situations in which the off-factor is expected to vary in the population of interest. The reason is that both are determined in part or in whole by the reduction in error associated with the off-factors.

Instead, we need either a particular set of summary statistics or an estimate of what MS_{within} would have been if the off-factors had not been included in the model. Glass et al. (1981) provided the following formula for estimation of the pooled standard deviation that would have resulted from a single factor design

$$\sigma = [(SS_B + SS_{AB} + SS_W)/(df_B + df_{AB} + df_W)]^{.5}, \quad (3.5)$$

where:

σ = pooled standard deviation,

SS_B = sum of squares for factor B, the other independent variable,

SS_{AB} = sum of squares for interaction term,

SS_W = sum of squares for within group (error term),

df_B = degrees of freedom for factor B,

df_{AB} = degrees of freedom for interaction term,

df_W = degrees of freedom for within group (error term).

The computed standard deviation is then used in Equation (1.2) to estimate the effect size.

In cases where neither means nor standard deviations are provided, the following formula derived by Morris and DeShon could be used to estimate the effect size:

$$d = g_a \left[(df_b + df_{ab} + df_e) / (df_b F_b + df_{ab} F_{ab} + df_e) \right]^{.5}, \quad (3.6)$$

where:

df_b = degrees of freedom for factor B,

df_{ab} = degrees of freedom for interaction term,

df_e = degrees of freedom for within group (crior term),

F_b = F statistic for factor B, $\qquad (3.7)$

F_{ab} = F statistic for interaction term,

$$g_a = \left\{ F_a \left[(n_{a1} + n_{a2}) / (n_{a1} n_{a2}) \right] \right\}^{.5},$$

where:

F_a = F statistic for factor A,

n_{a1} = sample size for level 1 of factor A,

n_{a2} = sample size for level 2 of factor A.

It should be noted that the use of the M & D procedure requires F statistics of fixed models. That is, in the ANOVA table, the F statistics should be computed using the following formula:

$$F_f = MS_i/MS_W, \qquad (3.8)$$

where

MS_i = mean square for factors or their interactions,

MS_W = mean square for the within group (error term).

If the studies use random or mixed models, the F statistics are calculated as follows for the random factors:

$$F_r = MS_i/MS_{AB}, \qquad (3.9)$$

where

MS_i = mean square for random factors,

MS_{AB} = mean square for the interaction term.

If studies report F_r (random F statistics), they should be transformed to F_f in order to use M & D procedures. The following formula can be used to transform F_r to F_f:

$$F_f = F_r * F_{AB}, \qquad (3.10)$$

where

F_{AB} = F statistic for interaction term.

Finally, for both the Glass and M & D procedures, "A" refers to the variable of interest in the particular analysis in question, while "B" refers to the other independent variable.

Example 3.1. Suppose that we are interested in computing an effect size value for the effect of watching a training video on performance on the ATC task. Suppose further that we have conducted a $2*2$ ANOVA with the dichotomous training video variable (TRNGVID1) as the independent variable of primary interest, gender as a second independent variable, and task performance (JOBPERF) as the dependent variable. The relevant summary statistics and ANOVA results are presented in Table 3.1. If the within cell means, standard deviations, and sample sizes were available, as they would be at the primary study level, then we might employ the N & G procedure to obtain an estimate of the effect size associated with the training video variable. First, we would use Equation (3.1) to generate the means that are to constitute the numerator of Equation (1.2).

$$\bar{x}_{i.} = (1/n_{i.}) \sum_{j=1}^{t} n_{ij} \bar{x}_{ij.},$$

$$\bar{x}_0 = (1/135)[(7.21*72) + (7.59*63)] = 7.39,$$

$$\bar{x}_1 = (1/165)[(8.99*96) + (8.89*69)] = 8.95.$$

TABLE 3.1
2 × 2 ANOVA Results

| | | Training Video | |
		0	1
G		Mean = 7.21	Mean = 8.99
e	0	Variance = 3.43	Variance = 5.94
n		n = 72	n = 96
d			
e		Mean = 7.59	Mean = 8.89
r	1	Variance = 1.94	Variance = 4.67
		n = 63	n = 69

| | | ANOVA Summary Table | | |
Source	df	SS	MS	F
Between cells	3	186.24		
Training	1	181.76	181.76	43.3
Gender	1	1.04	1.04	.25
Interaction	1	4.35	4.35	1.04
Within cells	296	1242.46	4.2	
Total	299	1428.7		

Then, we would use Equation (3.3) to generate the variance values that are to go into Equation (1.1)

$$\sigma_{i.}^2 = \left[\sum_{j=1}^{t} (n_{ij} - 1)\sigma_{ij}^2 + \sum_{j=1}^{t} n_{ij}(\bar{x}_{ij} - \bar{x}_{i.})^2 \right] \Bigg/ (n_{i.} - 1),$$

$$\sigma_0^2 = \{[(3.43 * 71) + (1.94 * 62)]$$

$$+ [(72 * -.18^2) + (63 * .20^2)]\}/134 = 2.75,$$

$$\sigma_1^2 = \{[(5.94 * 95) + (4.67 * 68)]$$

$$+ [(96 * .04^2) + (69 * -.06^2)]\}/164 = 5.41.$$

Thus,

$$s_p = \{[(134 * 2.75) + (164 * 5.41)]/298\}^{.5} = 2.05,$$

and

$$d = (8.95 - 7.39)/2.05 = .76.$$

Now, let us turn the tables a bit. If our focus were instead on the gender variable, then gender becomes the A variable and training video becomes the B variable. We must now decide whether or not the training video variable is "of theoretical interest." In other words, would we expect "exposure to a training video" to vary in the population to which we want to generalize?

Obviously, the training video variable is a manipulated variable in the present study, so one might argue that it would not vary in the population of interest. That is, in the population of interest, it is either the case that everyone is exposed to a training video or no one is exposed to a training video. In either case, there is no variability in exposure to a training video in the relevant population. Thus, the impact of the training video treatment should not be reflected in the denominator of the gender effect size value. As was explained previously, this is the simpler scenario since effect size would simply be the difference in gender means, computed using Equation (3.1), divided by the square root of the MS_{within} from the two-way ANOVA. Because of its simplicity, we need not take up space demonstrating this computation.[6] If instead the training video were expected to vary in the population to an extent similar to that produced in our experiment,[7] then the square root of the MS_{within} would be an underestimate of the denominator for the effect size computation. Instead, we might once again apply the N & G procedure. Then

$$\bar{x}_0 = (1/168)[(7.21*72) + (8.99*96)] = 8.23,$$

$$\bar{x}_1 = (1/132)[(7.59*63) + (8.89*69)] = 8.27,$$

$$\sigma_0^2 = \{[(3.43*71) + (5.95*95)]$$

$$+ [(72* - 1.02^2) + (96*.76^2)]\}/167 = 5.62,$$

$$\sigma_1^2 = \{[(1.94*62) + (4.67*68)]$$

$$+ [(63* - .68^2) + (69*.62^2)]\}/131 = 3.77,$$

$$s_p = \{[(167*5.62) + (131*3.77)]/298\}^{.5} = 2.19,$$

$$d = (8.23 - 8.27)/2.19 = -.018.$$

If within group standard deviations were unavailable, but sums of squares and degrees of freedom were, the Glass procedure for computing the pooled standard deviation could be combined with the N & G procedure for computing within group means to yield an alternative estimator. For the training video variable, we would have (from Equations (3.5) and (1.2)),

$$s_p = [(SS_B + SS_{AB} + SS_W)/(df_B + df_{AB} + df_W)]^{.5},$$

where A is the variable of primary interest in this analysis, namely, the training video variable, and B is the other variable, namely, gender. This formula yields

$$[(1.04 + 4.35 + 1242.46)/(1 + 1 + 296)]^{.5} = 2.05.$$

Thus,

$$d = 1.56/2.05 = .76.$$

For the gender variable (again assuming that the training video variable is of theoretical interest),

$$s_p = [(181.76 + 4.35 + 1242.46)/(1 + 1 + 296)]^{.5} = 2.19,$$

and

$$d = .04/2.19 = -.018.$$

Finally, if only F values and degrees of freedom are available instead of within group standard deviations for the training video calculations, we would have (from Equation (3.6)),

$$d = g_a[(df_b + df_{ab} + df_e)/(df_b F_b + df_{ab} F_{ab} + df_e)]^{.5},$$

where

$$g_a = [43.3(300/22275)]^{.5} = .76,$$

and thus,

$$d = .76[(1 + 1 + 296)/(.25 + 1.04 + 296)]^{.5} = .76.$$

For the gender variable,

$$g_a = [.03(300/22176)]^{.5} = .02,$$

and

$$d = .02[(1 + 1 + 296)/(43.3 + 1.036 + 296)]^{.5} = .018^8.$$

2 × k Factorial Design

In this type of factorial design, the first factor has two levels. The number of levels in the second factor can vary from 2 on up. In the previous section, we discussed estimation of effect size in a 2 × 2 factorial design. This section presents procedures for estimating effect size for situations in which the second factor has more than two levels.

As discussed in the previous section, there are three procedures that can be used in a 2 × 2 factorial design: Glass, M & D, and N & G. That is, all three of these procedures can be used to compute effect size values for effects with a single degree of freedom. In the 2 × k ≥ 3 case, the M & D and Glass procedures can only be used to compute effect size values for the term with two levels. Also, as always, they are typically most useful when primary data or relevant summary statistics are unavailable. The next section demonstrates each procedure in this context.

Example 3.2. Suppose we want to review previous studies that tested the hypothesis that field independence affects task performance. Further suppose that one of the studies examining this issue used a 2 × 3 factorial design. The first factor is a dichotomous variable indicating whether the individual was above or below the median on a measure of field independence (please disregard for the moment the problems associated with dichotomizing a continuous variable). The second factor was a trichotomous race variable indicating Whites, Hispanics, and Blacks. The JOBPERF variable was the dependent variable. Descriptive statistics and the ANOVA table for the hypothetical study are presented in Table 3.2.

Both independent variables in this example would presumably be expected to vary in the population to which we wish to generalize, so we do not concern ourselves here with computations involving the MS_{within}. It should simply be noted that there remains an assumption that the subgroup proportions in our study are similar to those found in the population to which we wish to generalize.

N & G Procedure. We use the descriptive statistics provided in Table 3.2 to estimate the performance effect size for high-field

TABLE 3.2

$2 \times k$ Factorial

	Field Independence	
	0	*1*
White	Mean = 9.41	Mean = 7.31
	Variance = 5.38	Variance = 1.93
	$n = 54$	$n = 45$
Hispanic	Mean = 8.41	Mean = 6.8
	Variance = 3.48	Variance = 4.62
	$n = 45$	$n = 57$
Black	Mean = 9.18	Mean = 8.39
	Variance = 4.12	Variance = 3.42
	$n = 48$	$n = 51$

	ANOVA Summary Table			
Source	*df*	*SS*	*MS*	*F*
Between cells	5			
Field independence	1	185.1	185.1	47.32
Race	2	90.0	45	11.5
Interaction	2	3.52	1.76	.45
Within cells	294	1150.08	3.91	
Total	299	1428.7		

independence versus low-field independence. Using Equations (3.1) and (3.3), we obtain

$$\bar{x}_{1.} = \left(1/n_{.j}\right) \sum_{i=1}^{g} n_{ij}\bar{x}_{ij}$$

$$= (1/150)[(45*7.31) + (57*6.80) + (48*8.39)] = 7.46,$$

$$\bar{x}_{2.} = \left(1/n_{.j}\right) \sum_{i=1}^{g} n_{ij}\bar{x}_{ij}$$

$$= (1/150)[(54*9.41) + (45*8.41) + (51*9.19)] = 9.03,$$

$$\sigma_{i.}^2 = \left[\sum_{j=1}^{t} (n_{ij} - 1)\sigma_{ij}^2 + \sum_{j=1}^{t} n_{ij}(\bar{x}_{ij} - \bar{x}_{i.})^2 \right] \Big/ (n_{i.} - 1),$$

$$\sigma_{1.}^2 = \left\{ \left[(45 - 1)(1.39)^2 + (57 - 1)(2.15)^2 + (48 - 1)(1.85)^2 \right. \right.$$

$$+ (45)(7.31 - 7.46)^2 + (57)(6.80 - 7.46)^2$$

$$\left. \left. + (48)(8.39 - 7.46)^2 \right] / (45 + 57 + 48 - 1) \right\}^{.5} = 3.84$$

$$\sigma_{2.}^2 = \left[(54 - 1)(2.32)^2 + (45 - 1)(1.87)^2 + (51 - 1)(2.03)^2 \right.$$

$$+ (54)(9.41 - 9.03)^2 + (45)(8.41 - 9.03)^2$$

$$\left. + (51)(9.19 - 9.03)^2 \right] / (54 + 45 + 51 - 1) = 4.49.$$

The pooled standard deviation can then be estimated using Equation (1.1) as follows:

$$s_p = \left\{ \left[(150 - 1)(3.84) + (150 - 1)(4.49) \right] / (150 + 150 - 2) \right\}^{.5}$$

$$= 2.04.$$

Using Equation (1.2), the effect size is

$$d = (9.03 - 7.46)/2.04 = 0.77.$$

Similarly we can estimate the performance effect size, for example, between Whites and Hispanics as follows:

$$\bar{x}_{1.} = (1/99) \left[(45 * 7.31) + (54 * 9.41) \right] = 8.46,$$

$$\bar{x}_{2.} = (1/102) \left[(57 * 6.80) + (45 * 8.41) \right] = 7.51,$$

$$\sigma_{1.}^2 = \left[(45 - 1)(1.39)^2 + (54 - 1)(2.32)^2 + (45)(7.31 - 8.46)^2 \right.$$

$$\left. + (54)(9.41 - 8.46)^2 \right] / (45 + 54 - 1) = 4.88,$$

$$\sigma_{2.}^2 = \left[(57 - 1)(2.15)^2 + (45 - 1)(1.87)^2 + (57)(6.80 - 7.51)^2 \right.$$

$$\left. + (45)(8.41 - 7.51)^2 \right] / (57 + 45 - 1) = 4.71.$$

The pooled standard deviation can then be estimated using Equation (1.1) as follows:

$$s_p = \{[(99 - 1)(4.88) + (102 - 1)(4.71)]/(99 + 102 - 2)\}^{.5}$$

$$= 2.19.$$

Using Equation (1.2), the effect size is

$$d = (8.46 - 7.51)/2.19 = 0.43.$$

Similar operations could be performed for the other two race comparisons.

Glass. The Glass procedure can be applied only to the two-level independent variable. Equation (3.5) gives us the pooled standard deviation that would have resulted from a single factor design

$$\sigma = [(SS_B + SS_{AB} + SS_W)/(df_B + df_{AB} + df_W)]^{.5}$$

$$= [(90 + 3.52 + 1150.08)/(2 + 2 + 294)]^{.5} = 2.04,$$

and this value forms the denominator of Equation (1.2). The numerator is found by applying the N & G procedure for obtaining group means from factorial designs as before:

$$\bar{x}_{1.} = (1/n_{.j}) \sum_{i=1}^{g} n_{ij}\bar{x}_{ij}$$

$$= (1/150)[(45*7.31) + (57*6.80) + (48*8.39)] = 7.46,$$

$$\bar{x}_{2.} = (1/n_{.j}) \sum_{i=1}^{g} n_{ij}\bar{x}_{ij}$$

$$= (1/150)[(54*9.41) + (45*8.41) + (51*9.19)] = 9.03.$$

Thus,

$$d = 1.57/2.04 = .77.$$

M & D. Like the Glass procedure, the M & D procedure can be applied only to the two-level variable. Using Equation (3.6),

$$d = g_a[(df_b + df_{ab} + df_e)/(df_b F_b + df_{ab} F_{ab} + df_e)]^{.5},$$

$$g_a = [47.32 * (300/22500)]^{.5} = .794,$$

$$d = .794 * [(2 + 2 + 294)/(23 + .9 + 294)]^{.5} = .77.$$

Finally, we caution once again against failing to consider the fixed versus the random nature of the ANOVA when applying this procedure.

$j \times k$ Factorial Design

In this type of factorial design, the number of levels in both factors vary from 2 on up. In previous sections, we discussed how to estimate effect size in 2×2 and $2 \times k$ factorial designs. In a $j \times k$ factorial design where $j, k \geq 3$, the only applicable procedure is the N & G procedure discussed earlier. Descriptive statistics would be used in precisely the same fashion as they were used in Examples 3.1 and 3.2.

Higher Order Factorial Designs. Many ANOVA designs have more than two factors. The most common of these is the three-way $(j \times k \times l)$ factorial design or three-way ANOVA. The number of levels in each factor can vary from 2 on up. In this section, we discuss procedures for estimating effect size for such higher-order factorial designs.

As with the $j \times k$ design, the Glass and M & D procedures can be applied only to those independent variables with two levels. Additionally, as always, the N & G procedure can be applied only when the appropriate summary statistics are available. In any case, application of the Glass and M & D procedures to the $j \times k \times l$ design involves expansion of Equations (3.5) and (3.6), respectively. For the Glass procedure, the equation for the pooled standard deviation becomes:

$$s_p = [(SS_B + SS_C + SS_{AB} + SS_{AC} + SS_{BC} + SS_{ABC} + SS_W)]/$$

$$[(df_B + df_C + df_{AB} + df_{AC} + df_{BC} + df_{ABC} + df_W)]^{.5}. \quad (3.11)$$

32

For the M & D procedure, d becomes:

$$d = g_a[(df_B + df_C + df_{AB} + df_{AC} + df_{BC} + df_{ABC} + df_e)/$$

$$(df_B F_B + df_C F_C + df_{AB} F_{AB}$$

$$+ df_{AC} F_{AC} + df_{BC} F_{BC} + df_{ABC} F_{ABC} + df_e)]^{.5}$$

$$= \{F_A[(n_{A1} + n_{A2})/(n_{A1} n_{A2})]\}^{.5}$$

$$\times [(df_B + df_C + df_{AB} + df_{AC} + df_{BC} + df_{ABC} + df_e)/$$

$$(df_B F_B + df_C F_C + df_{AB} F_{AB} + df_{AC} F_{AC}$$

$$+ df_{BC} F_{BC} + df_{ABC} F_{ABC} + df_e)]^{.5}. \tag{3.12}$$

Example 3.3. Suppose we want to review previous studies that tested the hypothesis that field independence affects task performance. Further suppose that one of the studies examining this issue used a $2 \times 3 \times 3$ factorial design. The first factor is a dichotomous variable indicating whether the individual was above or below the median on a measure of field independence. The second factor is a trichotomous race variable indicating Whites, Hispanics, and Blacks. The third factor is a trichotomous variable indicating the amount of caffeine that was given to subjects. Performance data were collected for subjects in each of the 18 groups. Descriptive statistics and ANOVA results are presented in Table 3.3.

It should first be noted that, while two of the independent variables in this example would certainly be expected to vary in the population and thus be of theoretical interest, it is unclear how we should treat the caffeine variable. Moreover, the resolution to this issue lies not in statistics but in the researcher's notions about the population to which results should generalize. For now, we treat this variable as if it were of theoretical interest. The issue of designs that contain both variables of theoretical interest and variables not of theoretical interest is taken up later.

TABLE 3.3
3-Way ANOVA

	Field Independence	
	0	*1*

Low caffeine:		
White	Mean = 8.64	Mean = 7.99
	Variance = 4.08	Variance = 3.17
	n = 21	n = 12
Hispanic	Mean = 8.56	Mean = 5.32
	Variance = 4.04	Variance = 2.34
	n = 9	n = 21
Black	Mean = 8.64	Mean = 8.34
	Variance = 3.1	Variance = 3.94
	n = 21	n = 18
Moderate caffeine:		
White	Mean = 8.14	Mean = 7.15
	Variance = 1.88	Variance = 2.04
	n = 9	n = 21
Hispanic	Mean = 8.94	Mean = 7.52
	Variance = 3.31	Variance = 3.53
	n = 18	n = 18
Black	Mean = 9.52	Mean = 8.46
	Variance = 7.07	Variance = 3.03
	n = 18	n = 15
High caffeine:		
White	Mean = 10.55	Mean = 6.93
	Variance = 5.66	Variance = .111
	n = 24	n = 12
Hispanic	Mean = 7.80	Mean = 7.81
	Variance = 3.10	Variance = 4.54
	n = 18	n = 18
Black	Mean = 9.63	Mean = 8.37
	Variance = 1.28	Variance = 3.68
	n = 12	n = 15

ANOVA Summary Table

Source	df	SS	MS	F
Between cells	17			
A: Field indep	1	185.1	185.1	52.84
B: Race	2	90.0	45	12.84
C: Caffeine	2	36.55	18.27	5.22
A × B	2	3.52	1.76	.50
A × C	2	0	0	0
B × C	4	94.53	23.63	6.75
A × B × C	4	34.63	8.66	2.47
Within cells	282	987.93	3.5	
Total	299	1428.7		

N & G Procedure. As before, the first step is to compute the means associated with the field independence variable. Then

$$\bar{x}_{1.} = (1/n_{.j}) \sum_{i=1}^{g} n_{ij}\bar{x}_{ij},$$

$$\bar{x}_{2.} = (1/n_{.j}) \sum_{i=1}^{g} n_{ij}\bar{x}_{ij},$$

$$\bar{x}_{1.} = (1/150)[(12*7.99) + (21*5.32) + (18*8.34) + (21*7.15)$$
$$+ (18*7.52) + (15*8.46) + (12*6.93)$$
$$+ (18*7.81) + (15*8.37)] = 7.46,$$

$$\bar{x}_{2.} = (1/150)[(21*8.64) + (9*8.56) + (21*8.64) + (9*8.14)$$
$$+ (18*8.94) + (18*9.52) + (24*10.55)$$
$$+ (18*7.81) + (12*9.63)] = 9.03,$$

$$\sigma_{i.}^2 = \left[\sum_{j=1}^{t} (n_{ij} - 1)\sigma_{ij}^2 + \sum_{j=1}^{t} n_{ij}(\bar{x}_{ij} - \bar{x}_{i.})^2 \right] \bigg/ (n_{i.} - 1),$$

$$\sigma_1^2 = \big[(12-1)(1.78)^2 + (21-1)(1.53)^2 + (18-1)(1.99)^2$$
$$+ (21-1)(1.43)^2 + (18-1)(1.88)^2 + (15-1)(1.74)^2$$
$$+ (12-1)(0.33)^2 + (18-1)(2.14)^2$$
$$+ (15-1)(1.92)^2$$
$$+ (12)(7.99 - 7.46)^2 + (21)(5.32 - 7.46)^2$$
$$+ (18)(8.34 - 7.46)^2 + (21)(7.15 - 7.46)^2$$
$$+ (18)(7.52 - 7.46)^2 + (15)(8.46 - 7.46)^2$$
$$+ (12)(6.93 - 7.46)^2 + (18)(7.81 - 7.46)^2$$
$$+ (15)(8.38 - 7.46)^2 \big] \bigg/$$
$$(12 + 21 + 18 + 21 + 18 + 15 + 12 + 18 + 15 - 1) = 3.84,$$

$$\sigma_2^2 = \big[(21 - 1)(2.02)^2 + (9 - 1)(2.01)^2 + (21 - 1)(1.76)^2$$
$$+ (9 - 1)(1.37)^2 + (18 - 1)(1.83)^2 + (18 - 1)(2.67)^2$$
$$+ (24 - 1)(2.38)^2 + (18 - 1)(1.76)^2 + (12 - 1)(1.13)^2$$
$$+ (21)(8.64 - 9.03)^2 + (9)(8.56 - 9.03)^2$$
$$+ (21)(8.64 - 9.03)^2 + (9)(8.14 - 9.03)^2$$
$$+ (18)(8.94 - 9.03)^2 + (18)(9.52 - 9.03)^2$$
$$+ (24)(10.55 - 9.03)^2 + (18)(7.81 - 9.03)^2$$
$$+ (12)(9.63 - 9.03)^2\big] /$$
$$(21 + 9 + 21 + 9 + 18 + 18 + 24 + 18 + 12 - 1) = 4.49.$$

The pooled standard deviation can then be estimated using Equation (1.1) as follows:

$$s_p = \{[(150 - 1)(3.84) + (150 - 1)(4.49)]/(150 + 150 - 2)\}^{.5}$$
$$= 2.04.$$

Using Equation (1.2), the effect size is

$$d = (9.03 - 7.46)/2.04 = 0.77.$$

Similarly we can estimate the performance effect size, for example, between Whites and Hispanics as follows:

$$\bar{x}_{1.} = (1/99)[(12 * 7.99) + (21 * 8.64) + (21 * 7.15)$$
$$+ (9 * 8.14) + (12 * 6.93) + (24 * 10.55)] = 8.46,$$
$$\bar{x}_{2.} = (1/102)[(21 * 5.32) + (9 * 8.56) + (18 * 7.52)$$
$$+ (18 * 8.94) + (18 * 7.81) + (18 * 7.81)] = 7.51,$$
$$\sigma_{1.}^2 = \big[(12 - 1)(1.78)^2 + (21 - 1)(2.02)^2 + (21 - 1)(1.43)^2$$
$$+ (9 - 1)(1.37)^2 + (12 - 1)(0.33)^2 + (24 - 1)(2.38)^2$$
$$+ (12)(7.99 - 8.46)^2 + (21)(8.64 - 8.46)^2$$

$$+ (21)(7.15 - 8.46)^2 + (9)(8.14 - 8.46)^2$$

$$+ (12)(6.93 - 8.46)^2 + (24)(10.55 - 8.46)^2] /$$

$$(12 + 21 + 21 + 9 + 12 + 24 - 1) = 4.88,$$

$$\sigma_{2.}^2 = \big[(21 - 1)(1.53)^2 + (9 - 1)(2.01)^2 + (18 - 1)(1.89)^2$$

$$+ (18 - 1)(1.83)^2 + (18 - 1)(2.14)^2 + (18 - 1)(1.76)^2$$

$$+ (21)(5.32 - 7.51)^2 + (9)(8.56 - 7.51)^2$$

$$+ (18)(7.52 - 7.51)^2 + (18)(8.94 - 7.51)^2$$

$$+ (18)(7.81 - 7.51)^2 + (18)(7.81 - 7.51)^2] /$$

$$(21 + 9 + 18 + 18 + 18 + 18 - 1) = 4.71.$$

The pooled standard deviation can then be estimated using Equation (1.1):

$$s_p = \big\{ [(n_{1.} - 1)s_{1.}^2 + (n_{2.} - 1)s_{2.}^2] / (n_{1.} + n_{2.} - 2) \big\}^{.5}$$

$$= \big\{ [(99 - 1)(4.88) + (102 - 1)(4.71)] / (99 + 102 - 2) \big\}^{.5}$$

$$= 2.19.$$

Using Equation (1.2), the effect size is

$$d = (8.46 - 7.51)/2.19 = 0.43.$$

Glass et al. Procedure. As discussed earlier, this approach is only relevant for the dichotomous field independence variable. The pooled standard deviation for field independence under this approach results in:

$$s = \big[(SS_B + SS_C + SS_{AB} + SS_{AC} + SS_{BC} + SS_{ABC} + SS_W)] /$$

$$[(df_B + df_C + df_{AB} + df_{AC} + df_{BC} + df_{ABC} + df_W)]^{.5}$$

$$= [(90 + 36.55 + 3.52 + 0.00 + 94.53 + 34.63 + 987.93) /$$

$$(2 + 2 + 2 + 2 + 4 + 4 + 284)]^{.5} = 2.04.$$

The pooled standard deviation would then serve as the denominator of Equation (1.2). The N & G procedure could then be applied to the within group means to yield a numerator for Equation (1.2), resulting in the same d value as the full N & G procedure.

M & D Procedure. The effect size for the field independence variable is estimated as follows (Morris & DeShon 1997, p. 194):

$$d = g_a[(df_B + df_C + df_{AB} + df_{AC} + df_{BC} + df_{ABC} + df_e)/$$
$$(df_B F_B + df_C F_C + df_{AB} F_{AB} + df_{AC} F_{AC}$$
$$+ df_{BC} F_{BC} + df_{ABC} F_{ABC} + df_e)]^{.5}$$

$$= \{F_A[(n_{A1} + n_{A2})/(n_{A1} n_{A2})]\}^{.5}$$
$$\times [(df_B + df_C + df_{AB} + df_{AC} + df_{BC} + df_{ABC} + df_e)/$$
$$(df_B F_B + df_C F_C + df_{AB} F_{AB} + df_{AC} F_{AC}$$
$$+ df_{BC} F_{BC} + df_{ABC} F_{ABC} + df_e)]^{.5}$$

$$= \{52.84[(150 + 150)/(150 \times 150)]\}^{.5}$$
$$\times \{(2 + 2 + 2 + 2 + 4 + 4 + 282)/$$
$$[(2)(12.84) + (2)(5.22) + (2)(.50)(2)(.00)$$
$$+ (4)(6.75) + (4)(2.47) + 282]\}^{.5} = .77.$$

As before, the fixed versus the random nature of the effects must be considered when applying this procedure. For lower-order designs, there exist simple formulas for converting random effect values to fixed effect values. These were presented earlier in the monograph. In a three-way design containing $k > 0$ random effect variables, conversion formulas are only available for some situations. These are presented in Table 3.4.

One final topic worth mentioning in this chapter has to do once again with the nature of the off-factors. Previously, we dealt with the two-way cases in which off-factor was and was not of theoretical interest. However, what if there are multiple off-factors, as in the $j \times k \times l$ design? The N & G, Glass, and M & D procedures can be used in situations where both of the off-factors are of theoretical interest. The square root of the MS_{within} can be used in the denomi-

TABLE 3.4
Transformation of Random F Test to Fixed F-Test Values from a Three-Way ANOVA

Source	F (A, B Fixed, C Random)	Transformation Formula	F (A, C Fixed, B Random)	Transformation Formula	F (B, C Fixed, A Random)	Transformation Formula
A	MS_A/MS_{AC}	$F_A * F_{AC}$	MS_A/MS_{AB}	$F_A * F_{AB}$	MS_A/MS_W	None
B	MS_B/MS_{BC}	$F_B * F_{BC}$	MS_B/MS_W	None	MS_B/MS_{AB}	$F_B * F_{AB}$
C	MS_C/MS_W	None	MS_C/MS_{BC}	$F_A * F_{BC}$	MS_C/MS_{AC}	$F_C * F_{AC}$
$A * B$	MS_{AB}/MS_{ABC}	$F_{AB} * F_{ABC}$	MS_{AB}/MS_W	None	MS_{AB}/MS_W	None
$A * C$	MS_{AC}/MS_W	None	MS_{AC}/MS_{ABC}	$F_{AC} * F_{ABC}$	MS_{AC}/MS_W	None
$B * C$	MS_{BC}/MS_W	None	MS_{BC}/MS_W	None	MS_{BC}/MS_{ABC}	$F_{BC} * F_{ABC}$
$A * B * C$	MS_{ABC}/MS_W	None	MS_{ABC}/MS_W	None	MS_{ABC}/MS_W	None

MS_W = Mean square for within group (error term).

nator of the effect size formula when both off-factors are not of theoretical interest. Now suppose that one off-factor *is* expected to vary freely in the population of interest while the other off-factor is not. There was some question as to whether Example 3.3 was such a case. In such a case, the N & G, Glass, and M & D procedures will result in an overestimate of error while the square root of MS_{within} will result in an underestimate of error. This is not a simple problem, and there is no commonly (or even uncommonly) accepted solution. However, we would suggest a modification of the Glass or M & D procedures. For example, Equation (3.11) involves nothing more than the addition of sums of squares associated with two off-factors and interactions to the three-way, MS_{within}. The same is done with degrees of freedom. However, suppose that factor *C* were not of theoretical interest. In such a case, we might use a partial version of Equation (3.11), such as

$$s = \left[(SS_B + SS_{AB} + SS_W)\right] / \left[(df_B + df_{AB} + df_W)\right]^{.5}.$$

That is, we might remove from Equation (3.11) the terms containing the off-factor that is not of theoretical interest. The result is simply Equation (3.5) from the two-way case.

Similar modifications might be made to Equation (3.12) to reach the same end, namely, Equation (3.6). We would, however, caution the reader that research needs to be conducted to confirm that such modifications result in reasonable estimates of the pooled standard deviation that would have resulted from a one-way design.

Summary

In this chapter, we demonstrated the complications introduced to computation of effect size values by additional independent variables. One procedure was described for the case in which off-factors were not of theoretical interest, while three procedures were described for the case in which the opposite is true. The Nouri and Greenberg (1995) procedure is applied to summary statistics for any independent groups variable. The Glass et al. (1981) and Morris and DeShon (1997) procedures are applied to ANOVA summary table values pertaining to dichotomous variables. In those situations to which all three procedures can be applied, they should result in the same value.

4. ANCOVA DESIGNS

So far, we have dealt only with the typical ANOVA design in which the antecedent variables are categorical. Oftentimes, however, we wish to examine the effect of an independent variable on a dependent variable while holding a continuous variable constant. Consider the field independence example used in the demonstration of effect size computations for the two independent groups design. There, we examined the effect of the categorical field independence variable on the task performance variable and found a d value of .77.

However, field independence has been shown to overlap with cognitive ability, and it might be that we wish to examine the effect of field independence on task performance while holding cognitive ability constant. In such a case, ANCOVA might be used. Of course, one may wish for the effect size value that results from such an analysis to reflect the overlap between the dependent variable and independent variable with the covariate held constant.

Arvey, Cole, Hazucha, and Hartanto (1985) drew on the work of Cohen (1977) to derive a formula for computing d from a two-group ANCOVA design. We must begin with the standard formula for d as represented by Arvey et al. (1985), $d = (Y_{\text{bar}-E} - Y_{\text{bar}-C})/s_y$, where the numerator is the difference between the experimental and control group means. In the ANCOVA design, we are dealing with partial values. Thus, the mean values are in fact means for the two groups with the covariate held constant. Arvey et al. (1985) therefore rewrite the d formula as:

$$d = (Y'_{\text{bar}-E} - Y'_{\text{bar}-C})/s_{y'}, \qquad (4.1)$$

where $Y'_{\text{bar}-E}$ and $Y'_{\text{bar}-C}$ are the dependent variable means for the experimental and control groups with the covariate held constant.

Cohen (1977) offers the following formula for Y':

$$Y' = Y - b(X - X_{\text{bar}}), \qquad (4.2)$$

where X is the covariate, X_{bar} is its mean, and b is the weight from the regression of Y onto the covariate. Thus, the numerator of

Equation (4.1) can be rewritten as:

$$[Y_E - b_E(X_E - X_{\text{bar}-E})]_{\text{bar}-E} - [Y_C - b_C(X_C - X_{\text{bar}-C})]_{\text{bar}-C}.$$
$$(4.3)$$

However, Arvey et al. (1985) point out that if we assume equality of subgroup covariate means, then this formula can be simplified. Such an assumption is not likely to be problematic given random assignment of subjects to treatments. However, the assumption may be more tenuous for naturally occurring variables such as gender. This topic is taken up later in this chapter. In any case, even without random assignment, there are many situations in which there is no reason to suspect a relationship between the independent variable and the covariate. If we can make such an assumption about the covariate means, and if we also assume that the weights from the regression of the dependent variable onto the covariate are equal for the subgroups (a common assumption of ANCOVA), then $b_E(X_E - X_{\text{bar}-E}) = b_C(X_C - X_{\text{bar}-C})$ and Equation (4.3) reduces to

$$Y_{\text{bar}-E} - Y_{\text{bar}-C},$$

which is once again the difference between the subgroup means. If either of these assumptions is untenable, then Equation (4.3) must be used.

At this point, there are two options. The choice of options depends once again on the population to which one wishes to generalize. Consider that a covariate is typically a variable that occurs naturally. It might, therefore, be considered a variable of theoretical interest. If so, then one can use the ordinary pooled standard deviation, computed using Equations (1.1), (3.3), etc. as before to compute effect size. That is, one can use the standard deviation that would have resulted without removal of the covariate. In interpreting ANCOVA results, however, one is often particularly interested in the standardized magnitude of effect holding the nuisance–covariate constant. To this end, we often wish to use not only the covariate adjusted means, but also the covariate adjusted standard deviation. This can be useful not only at the individual ANCOVA study level but also at the meta-analytic level. Consider that there are many areas of inquiry in which certain variables, often demographic variables like SES, are routinely held constant. In such cases, meta-analysis might be performed on the relationships between certain variables holding a particular third variable constant. If so, then the denominator of the effect size statistic must reflect this adjustment. In the pages that follow, we explain how this can be accomplished. It should be noted, however, that this represents a departure from our definition of effect size as a value that would have resulted from a simple one-way design.

Effect Size Holding the Covariate Constant

Arvey et al. (1985) show that, if we add an additional assumption that the variances of the dependent variable and covariate are equal to one another, then the denominator of Equation (4.1) can be expressed in terms of the standard deviation of the dependent variable and the correlation between the covariate and the dependent variable as follows

$$s_{y'} = s_y\left(1 - r_{XY}^2\right)^{.5}, \tag{4.4}$$

where s_y is simply the standard deviation of the dependent variable. Although pooling was unnecessary in their example because they assumed equal subgroup variances, the pooled standard deviation (instead of the standard deviation of the dependent variable) would be appropriate when this assumption is not likely to be met. Thus, Equation (4.4) might be better represented as:

$$s_{p'} = s_p\left(1 - r_{XY}^2\right)^{.5}, \tag{4.5}$$

where s_p is calculated with Equation (1.1), and $s_{p'}$ is the pooled standard deviation with the covariate held constant. Thus, $s_{p'}$ serves as the denominator of Equation (4.1).

Unfortunately, a transcription error in the 1985 article resulted in the omission of the exponent for the correlation term.[9] Although the formula is represented correctly later in the Arvey et al. (1985) paper, the omission was repeated in later work (e.g., Arvey & Cole, 1989). In any case, what remains is the following formula for the effect size index representing the strength of the relationship between the independent and dependent variables with the covariate held constant. Thus,

$$(Y_{\text{bar}-E} - Y_{\text{bar}-C})\big/\left[s_p(1 - r_{XY}^2)^{.5}\right]. \tag{4.6}$$

One problem that should be pointed out is that the assumption of equal covariate and dependent variable variances is not often met. Neither can this problem be resolved simply by standardizing the variables in the analysis. Those who are not convinced of this need only plug the relevant values into Equations (4.6) and (4.7) (which is described below). This does not affect the numerator of Equation (4.1), but it does cause a slightly more complicated denominator. Specifically, the denominator must be expressed in terms of the pooled variance, the covariate variance, the covariance between the covariate and the dependent variable, and the unstandardized regression weight from the regression of the dependent variable onto the covariate. This more general form of Equation (4.6) is

$$(Y_{\text{bar}-E} - Y_{\text{bar}-C})\big/\left[s_p^2 + b^2 s_X^2 - 2b\,\text{COV}_{XY}\right]^{.5}, \tag{4.7}$$

where the numerator contains simple subgroup means and the denominator contains the pooled variance as calculated with Equation (1.1), the weight (squared and not squared) from the regression of the dependent variable onto the covariate, and the covariance between the covariate and the dependent variable.

Example 4.1. Let us now return to the example mentioned earlier in which we wish to examine the effect of field independence on task performance with intelligence treated as a covariate. Because the intelligence (IQ1) and task performance variables have vastly different variances on expectation, we use Equation (4.7) to compute effect size. Thus, the values that are needed are the subgroup dependent variable means, the dependent variable variance (or pooled variance if the subgroup variances are unequal), the covariate variance, and the unstandardized weight from the regression of the dependent variable onto the covariate. See Table 4.1.

The high-field independence group had a dependent variable mean of 9.03, while the low group had a mean of 7.46. The variance of the covariate was 255.04, the pooled dependent variable variance was 4.17, the unstandardized weight from the regression of the dependent variable onto the covariate was 0.053, and the covariance between

TABLE 4.1

Two-Group Comparison with One Covariate

High-field independence mean = 9.03

Low-field independence mean = 7.46

Pooled variance $(s_p^2) = \{[(N_1 - 1)s_1^2 + (N_2 - 1)s_2^2]/[N_1 + N_2 - 2]\}$

$\qquad = [(149*3.84) + (149*4.53)]/298 = 4.17$

$s_{IQ}^2 = 255.04$

$b_{y.IQ} = .053$

$COV_{y.IQ} = 13.503$

$d = (Y_E - Y_C)/[s_p^2 + b^2 s_X^2 - 2b\,COV_{XY}]^5$

$\qquad = [9.03 - 7.46]/[4.17 + .053^2 * 255.04 - 2*.053*13.503]^5 = .84$

---

the dependent variable and the covariate was 13.50. Thus, the d value representing the magnitude of the relationship between field independence and task performance with intelligence held constant is

$$(Y_{bar-E} - Y_{bar-C})/\left[s_p^2 + b^2 s_X^2 - 2b\,COV_{XY}\right]^{.5},$$

$$[9.03 - 7.46]/[4.17 + .053^2 * 255.04 - 2*.053*13.50]^{.5} = .84.$$

Thus, it appears that the holding constant of intelligence had a slight positive impact (from .77 to .84) on the effect size associated with the relationship between field independence and task performance.[10] These computations are simple enough if one is basing them on a complete primary data set. However, complications are likely to arise if such computations are to be based on the numbers reported in published work, as is often the case in meta-analysis. If it happens that the dependent variable and covariate variances are equal, then all that is needed to compute an effect size index is the subgroup means, the dependent variable standard deviation (or pooled standard deviation), and the correlation between the dependent variable and the covariate. These values can then be plugged into Equation (4.6) to obtain a d value. If the dependent variable and covariate variances are not equal, then all of the values contained in Equation (4.7) must be reported (or otherwise available) in order to compute the effect size index.

Other ANCOVA Designs

ANCOVA with More than Two Groups

At this point, it might be useful to bring together some of the material in this chapter with some of the material in Chapters 2 and 3. The procedures for computing effect size values from two-group designs can be expanded to include those designs that contain more than two groups.

Equation (4.7), which relies on assumptions of equal subgroup covariate means and regression weights, contains the subgroup means, a pooled dependent variable variance value, the weight from the regression of the dependent variable onto the covariate, and the covariate variance. Equations (3.1) or (3.2) can be used to find the mean values that comprise the numerator of Equation (4.7). Likewise, Equations (3.3) or (3.4) can be used to find the subgroup variance values that go into the pooled variance value. Finally, the regression weight and covariate variance values are obtained as before.

Example 4.2. Suppose that we are interested in estimating the magnitude of the difference in task performance between ATCs using the continuous motion screen display and the 5 s update screen display while holding cognitive ability constant. The two levels of our antecedent variable are, in fact, embedded within an independent variable with three levels. Thus, we must use only the means and dependent variable variability values of the groups of interest. These values are then inserted into Equation (4.7) the relevant correlation, regression weight, and variance values for the covariate into the equation to ascertain the desired d value. See Table 4.2.

Mean task performance is 8.28 for the continuous display group and 8.48 for the 5 s interval group, resulting in a mean difference of $-.2$. Variances for the two groups were 3.97 and 5.21, respectively. Using Equation (1.1),

$$s_p = \left\{ \left[(N_1 - 1)s_1^2 + (N_2 - 1)s_2^2 \right] / \left[N_1 + N_2 - 2 \right] \right\}^{.5},$$

we ascertain a pooled standard deviation value of 2.14 and a pooled variance of 4.59.

TABLE 4.2

One-Way ANCOVA with $k > 2$ Levels

Continuous display mean = 8.28
5 s update mean = 8.48
$s_1^2 = 3.97$
$s_2^2 = 5.21$
$s_p^2 = \{[(N_1 - 1)s_1^2 + (N_2 - 1)s_2^2]/[N_1 + N_2 - 2]\} = 4.59$
$b_{Y.IQ} = .053$
$COV_{Y.IQ} = 13.503$
$d = (8.28 - 8.48)/[4.59 + (.053^2 * 255.04) - (2 * .053 * 13.503)]^{.5}$
$\quad = -.2/(3.87)^{.5} = -.101$
If conscientiousness is added as a second covariate, we need:
$b_{IQ} = .05, b_{CONS} = .21, COV_{IQ.CONS} = 3.92, COV_{Y.CONS} = .42$
Thus,
$s_{p'} = [4.59 + (.05^2 * 255.04) + (.21^2 * 1.1) + (2 * .05 * .21 * 3.92)$
$\quad - (2 * .05 * 13.5) - (2 * .21 * .42)]^{.5} = 1.96$
$d = -.24/1.96 = -.12$

These values can then be plugged into Equation (4.7) along with the weight from the regression of the dependent variable onto the covariate and the variance of the covariate. These values are .053 and 13.50, respectively. Thus, the d formula, with all values plugged in, is

$$(8.28 - 8.48)/\left[4.59 + (.053^2 * 255.04) - (2 * .05 * 13.50)\right]^{.5}$$

$$= -.2/(3.87)^{.5} = -.101.$$

It is important to note that, because the denominator contains only a function of within group variances (i.e., the pooled variance) and values involving the covariate and its bivariate relationship with the dependent variable, the presence of the third display category has no impact on any portion of the denominator other than the within group variances. It is only the numerator that requires special consideration.

Higher-Order ANCOVAs

In the case of one-way ANCOVA, the values in the numerator are easily calculated from summary statistics. With higher-order ANCOVAs, the N & G procedure can be used to extract information relevant for the comparison of interest. These values then comprise the numerator of Equation (4.7), and once again, the denominator is unaffected by the presence of the additional factors. We remind the reader once again that the N & G procedure is appropriate if the off-factors are of theoretical interest. If the covariate is also to be treated as a variable of theoretical interest, then the procedure for covariate adjustment described above should not be used.

Effect Size for ANCOVA with Multiple Covariates

To compute the effect size for the relationship between an independent variable and a dependent variable with multiple variables covaried out, the denominator of Equation (4.7) must be expanded. Given the assumptions of equal covariate means across subgroups and equal weights for the regression of the dependent variable onto covariates across subgroups, the numerator is still simply the difference between means. We present the denominator formula for the two covariate case. While this could be expanded further to accommodate $k > 2$ covariates, the equation grows exponentially with the addition of covariates since it must include (multiple times) all weights from the regression of the dependent variable onto the covariates, all covariate variances, all covariances between the dependent variable and each of the covariates, and all covariances among the covariates themselves.

For the two covariate case, the equation for the denominator of the d formula is

$$\left\{ s_p^2 + b_1^2 s_{X1}^2 + b_2^2 s_{X2}^2 + 2b_1 b_2 \, \text{COV}(X_1, X_2) \right.$$

$$\left. - 2b_1 \, \text{COV}(X_1, Y) - 2b_2 \, \text{COV}(X_2, Y) \right\}^{.5}, \qquad (4.8)$$

where the s^2 values are variances for the dependent variable (pooled) and each of the two covariates, the b values are the weights from the regression of the dependent variable onto the covariates, and the COV values are the covariances among the dependent variable, the first covariate, and the second covariate. (Derivation for the formula is provided in Appendix B.)

If we wished to add conscientiousness to Example 4.2 as a second covariate, then computation of Equation (4.8) would require the pooled dependent variable variance, the weights from the regression of the dependent variable onto each of the covariates, the covariate variances, and the three covariances among the covariates and the dependent variable. Equation (4.8) then yields a denominator value of

$$s_{p'} = \left[4.59 + (.05^2 * 255.04) + (.21^2 * 1.1) + (2 * .05 * .21 * 3.92) \right.$$
$$\left. - (2 * .05 * 13.5) - (2 * .21 * .42)\right]^{.5} = 1.96,$$

which, when plugged into Equation (4.7), yields a d value of $-.12$. Thus, the addition of conscientiousness as a covariate had very little impact on effect size.

Before concluding this chapter, we feel it is important to revisit the assumptions of equal subgroup regression weights and covariate means mentioned earlier. If subjects are randomly assigned to groups, then these assumptions should not be problematic, and the numerators of Equations (4.6) and (4.7) may remain the same. However, there are many cases in which there is every reason to believe that one or both of these assumptions are not met. The developmental psychology literature offers the example of comparisons across grades with age held constant.[11] Clearly, the assumption of equal subgroup covariate means is untenable. As a result, the numerator of Equation (4.1) no longer reduces to the simple difference between dependent variable means. Instead, the numerator of Equation (4.1) must be Equation (4.3) in its entirety. It should be apparent that, while this poses no problem for the researcher who possesses the raw data, it virtually eliminates the possibility of computing effect size for the researcher who is working from the published report. Thus, if the assumptions of equal covariate means and regression weights are untenable, and if the raw data are unavailable, effect size incorporating the covariate(s) cannot be computed from published reports.

Summary

In this chapter, we showed that the introduction of covariates to an ANOVA design produces unique difficulties. The procedures developed by Arvey and his colleagues were then demonstrated. This procedure was further expanded to accommodate less restrictive assumptions, $k > 2$ levels of the independent variable, multiple independent variables, and multiple covariates.

5. REPEATED MEASURES DESIGNS

Repeated measures designs are often used because of the statistical power that they offer relative to independent groups designs. These designs allow for the removal of the variance associated with individual differences from error terms, thus decreasing the denominator of common test statistics such as t and F. The problem is that, if such test statistics are converted into effect size values without consideration of the repeated measures nature of the design, effect size values are inflated (Dunlap, Cortina, Vaslow, and Burke, 1996).

Recall that the effect size, d, for a two-group design is found by dividing the difference in group means by the control or pooled standard deviation. This is the correct formula for computing d from summary statistics *regardless of the type of design* (i.e., repeated measures vs. independent groups). That is, it makes no difference whether the values in the two groups come from the same people or from two different sets of people, the effect size is what it is. Let us state this using our prior terminology. Unlike other off-factors, subject differences are always of theoretical interest in the sense that they are always expected to be present in the population to which we wish to generalize. Thus, variability due to differences between subjects must be present in the denominator of the effect size estimator.

When computing effect size values from test statistics, the difference in design can be critical. Equation (1.5) provides the formula for computing d values from t values from independent groups designs. However, to the extent that the measure-to-measure correlation is greater than zero, the t value from the repeated measures design is larger than the value from the independent groups design. It is precisely this correlation that gives the repeated measures design its power advantage, but this power advantage has nothing to do with the size of the effect. In other words, the repeated measures t value must be corrected downward according to the level of measure-to-measure correlation before the d value can be computed from such test statistics.

The formula for computing d from a repeated measures t is[12]

$$d = t_r \{ [(1 - r)/n_1] + [(1 - r)/n_2] \}^{.5}, \qquad (5.1)$$

where r is the correlation between the measures and n_i is the samples size for measure i.
For equal n,

$$d = t_r[2(1 - r)/n]^{.5}. \qquad (5.2)$$

As can be seen, the only difference between the formula for converting the independent groups t and the formula for converting the repeated measures t is that, in the repeated measures formula, the numerator of the ratio is reduced by r, the correlation between measures. It should also be noted that Equations (5.1) and (5.2) apply equally well to other types of two-group, correlated measure designs such as the matched groups design and the gain score design.

Example 5.1. Suppose we are interested in computing an effect size value for the effect of target speed 1 versus target speed 2 on task performance when the number of targets is low. In the table in Appendix A, these would be the NUM1SP1 and NUM1SP2 columns. For the sake of simplicity, we treat these two levels as if they were the only two levels of the target speed variable. Thus, we wish to obtain the effect size value corresponding to the difference in task performance associated with a change in target speed from 1 mm/s to 5 mm/s. See Table 5.1.

The mean for the first group is 7.999, the mean for the second group is 7.806, and the pooled standard deviation is 2.05. Calculating d directly from Equation (1.2), we obtain a value of .094. The

TABLE 5.1
Two-Group Repeated Measures Design

1 mm/s mean = 7.999
5 mm/s mean = 7.806
s_p = 2.05
$d = (7.999 - 7.806)/2.05 = .094$
$t_r = 1.372$
$d = t_r\{[(1 - r)/n_1] + [(1 - r)/n_2]\}^{.5} = 1.372\{[(1 - .298)/300] + [(1 - .298)/300]\}^{.5}$
  $= .094$
$d = t_I[(1/n_1) + (1/n_2)]^{.5} = 1.15[2/300]^{.5} = .094$
$\sigma_d^2 = [2(1 - r)/n] + [d^2/(2n - 2)] = [2(.702)/300] + [.094^2/(300)] = .00936$

repeated measures t value can also be used to find d. The repeated measures t in this case is 1.372 which, when plugged into Equation (5.1), yields once again a d value of .094. Note also that, if these repeated measures data were analyzed with an independent groups t test, the corresponding t value would be 1.15. When plugged into the formula for converting independent groups t values into d values (Equation (1.5)), this also yields a d value of .094. The trick is that, if we plug the repeated measures t value into the formula for converting independent groups t values into d values, we get the incorrect value of .112. Moreover, this discrepancy becomes more pronounced as the true d value increases.

This is worth noting for two reasons. First, while the equation for converting independent groups t values into d values is well known, the equation for converting repeated measures t values is not. Indeed, Dunlap et al. (1996) were unable to find the formula anywhere in the literature and derived it themselves. Second, as discussed in the Dunlap et al. (1996) article, common sources for such information either ignore this problem or give misleading information. This has resulted in miscalculations of effect sizes in quite a few studies (see Dunlap et al., 1996 for a detailed discussion of these issues). The lesson is that repeated measures test statistics must be treated differently from independent groups test statistics when computing indices of effect size from test statistics instead of from summary statistics.

Finally, it is worth noting that it is also possible to compute effect sizes from such a two-group, repeated measures design by using a modified version of the M & D procedure. This is accomplished by treating the "subjects" variable as a second independent variable and applying Equation (3.6) (Morris & DeShon's Equation (9)). The catch is that no test on the subjects X treatment interaction is possible because the effect lacks an error term. Thus, Equation (3.6) can be modified as follows:

$$d = g_a [(df_b + df_e)/(df_b F_b + df_e)]^{.5}, \qquad (5.3)$$

where: df_b is the degrees of freedom for the subjects term, F_b is the ratio of mean squares subjects to mean squares residual, and df_e is the degrees of freedom residual.

For Example 5.1, the g_a value is

$$g_a = [(1.88 * (600/90000)]^{.5} = .112,$$

and thus,

$$d = .112\{(299 + 299)/[(299 * 1.83) + 299]\}^{.5} = .094.$$

Higher-Order Repeated Measures Designs

Not surprisingly, the situation is a bit more complicated for designs involving multiple effects, at least one of which is a repeated measures variable. This is particularly true if one wishes to extract an effect size value for two of $k > 2$ levels of one of the independent variables.

The complications arise whenever one must collapse across rows or columns whose values are correlated with one another. In such a case, this correlation must be taken into account.

Example 5.2. Suppose we are once again interested in the effect of the 1 mm/s target speed versus the 5 mm/s target speed on task performance when the number of targets is low. Unlike the previous example, we suppose that this comparison involves two of the three levels of the speed variable, 10 mm/s being the third. Additionally, suppose this repeated measures independent variable is accompanied by a second, independent groups variable, namely, gender.

The computation of effect size for any two of the three levels of the repeated measures target speed variable can be done with the same N & G procedure that we saw in the factorial ANOVA portions of Chapter 3.[13] That is, we use Equations (3.1) or (3.2) to compute group means, Equations (3.3) or (3.4) to compute group variances, plug the variances into Equation (1.1) to get the pooled variance, then plug this value and the difference between means into Equation (1.2). Thus, for the 1 mm/s versus 5 mm/s comparison, we would compute the following

$$\bar{x}_{1.} = (1/n_{.j}) \sum_{i=1}^{g} n_{ij}\bar{x}_{ij} = (1/300)[(168 * 7.93) + (132 * 8.09)]$$

$$= 7.99,$$

$$\bar{x}_{2.} = (1/n_{.j}) \sum_{i=1}^{g} n_{ij}\bar{x}_{ij} = (1/300)\left[(168 * 7.7) + (132 * 7.94)\right]$$

$$= 7.80,$$

$$\sigma_{1.}^2 = \left[\sum_{j=1}^{t} (n_{ij} - 1)\sigma_{ij}^2 + \sum_{j=1}^{t} n_{ij}(\bar{x}_{ij} - \bar{x}_{i.})^2\right]\bigg/(n_{i.} - 1)$$

$$= \{(167 * 5.0) + (131 * 4.64) + (168 * .004) + (132 * .01)\}/299$$

$$= 4.83,$$

$$\sigma_{2.}^2 = \{(167 * 3.12) + (131 * 4.14) + (168 * .01) + (132 * .02)\}/299$$

$$= 3.57,$$

$$s_p = 2.05,$$

$$d = (7.99 - 7.8)/2.05 = .094.$$

However, the situation is different for the independent groups variable in this design. Because the measurements in any given row of Table 5.2 are correlated, this correlation must be taken into account when computing values for the independent groups variable. Thus, different equations must be used to compute effect size (Nouri & Greenberg, 1995).

TABLE 5.2

The 3 * 3 Mixed ANOVA Design

			Target Speed	
		1 mm/s	5 mm/s	10 mm/s
0	Mean =	7.93	7.70	7.15
	Var. =	5.0	3.12	4.26
	Std. dev. =	2.24	1.77	2.06
	$r_{11,12} = .183, r_{11,13} = .339, r_{12,13} = .339^*$			
1	Mean =	8.09	7.94	7.26
	Var. =	4.64	4.14	3.95
	Std. dev. =	2.15	2.03	1.99
	$r_{21,22} = .428, r_{21,23} = .277, r_{22,23} = .489^*$			

* Correlations between performance at times 1 and 2, times 1 and 3, and times 2 and 3.

54

First, means are calculated using the following formula:

$$\bar{x}_{i.} = \sum_{j=1}^{t} \bar{x}_{ij}, \qquad (5.4)$$

where the values are as before. Note that the "means" necessary for implementation of the Nouri and Greenberg (1995) procedure are, in fact sums of means. We refer the reader to the original source for a more detailed discussion of this formula.

Within group variances are then computed with the following:

$$\sigma_{i.}^2 = \sum_{j=1}^{t} \sigma_{ij}^2 + 2 \sum_{j=1}^{t} \rho_{ij, ij+m} \sigma_{ij} \sigma_{ij+m}, \qquad (5.5)$$

where σ_{ij}^2 once again represents within cell variances, $\rho_{ij, ij+m}$ represents the correlation between the values in cell ij and cell $ij + m$, and σ_{ij+m} represents the standard deviation of the values in the latter of these cells.

Thus, returning to Example 5.2, suppose we wish to compute effect size for the gender variable. Group means are computed as

$$\bar{x}_{1.} = \sum_{j=1}^{t} \bar{x}_{ij} = 7.93 + 7.7 + 7.15 = 22.78,$$

$$\bar{x}_{2.} = \sum_{j=1}^{t} \bar{x}_{ij} = 8.09 + 7.94 + 7.26 = 23.29.$$

Within group variances are computed as:

$$\sigma_{1.}^2 = \sum_{j=1}^{t} \sigma_{ij}^2 + 2 \sum_{j=1}^{t} \rho_{ij, ij+m} \sigma_{ij} \sigma_{ij+m}$$

$$= 5 + 3.12 + 4.26 + 2(.183)(2.24)(1.77)$$

$$+ 2(.339)(2.24)(2.06) + 2(.339)(1.77)(2.06)$$

$$= 19.43,$$

$$\sigma_{2.}^2 = 4.64 + 4.14 + 3.95 + 2(.428)(2.15)(2.03)$$

$$+ 2(.277)(2.15)(1.99) + 2(.489)(2.03)(1.99)$$

$$= 22.78.$$

The pooled standard deviation is then computed by plugging these last two values into Equation (1.1). It should be noted, however, that the ns in Equation (1.1) refer to the number of subjects and not to the number of values. Thus,

$$s_p = \{[(167 * 19.43) + (131 * 22.78)]/298\}^{.5} = 4.57,$$

and

$$d = (23.29 - 22.78)/4.57 = .111.$$

Computing Sampling Error Variance of Effect Sizes

We mentioned earlier that the computation of sampling error variances for d values is fairly straightforward for most designs and involves only the sample size and the d value in question. This is not true when d values come from repeated measures designs (or any design that results in nonzero measure to measure correlations). In such cases, the sampling error variance of d is partly a function of the degree to which the measure to measure correlation differs from zero.

Becker (1988) offered the following formula for σ_e^2 from such designs

$$\sigma_e^2 = [2(1 - r)/n] + [d^2/(2n - 2)], \qquad (5.6)$$

where n is the within group sample size and r is the correlation between measures. For the above example, this sampling error variance value is .00936. It is worth noting that the value resulting from the Hunter and Schmidt formula is .01344. The lack of difference here is not surprising. Dunlap et al. (1996) showed that the difference in the values produced by the two formulas is always small and disappears before the third decimal place for studies with reasonable sample sizes (e.g., > 50) or moderate to large correlations between measures.

While these test statistic-based computations are straightforward at the primary study level, they can be more complicated at the meta-analytic level. The reason for this is that correlations between measures in repeated measures designs are often not reported. If this is the case (and if effect size cannot be computed directly from means and standard deviations), then there are two options. The first is to exclude the study from the meta-analysis. The second alternative is to impute a measure-to-measure correlation value based on the existing literature. In other words, previous empirical research may suggest a measure-to-measure correlation value for the variable in question. If a reasonable estimate can be made, then d can be estimated from Equation (5.1) above. A potentially useful line of future research would be to meta-analyze correlations between measures, broken down by relevant moderator variables, in an attempt to provide other researchers conducting meta-analyses with trustworthy estimates of correlation values that can be used to convert repeated measures t values into d values.

Summary

In this chapter, we showed that the nonzero correlations between measures in repeated measures, matched groups, and gain score designs create unique complications. Indeed, a lack of consideration of these correlations has caused computation and interpretation problems in the past. We then showed that while the computations from summary statistics for a two-group repeated measures design are not complicated, computations from test statistics are less clear. Further difficulties are associated with the introduction of additional groups and variables. It was shown that variations of the Nouri and Greenberg procedure can be applied in such situations.

6. MONOGRAPH SUMMARY AND DISCUSSION OF ANCILLARY ISSUES

Summary

The primary purpose of this monograph was to review and demonstrate procedures for computing effect size values in various ANOVA designs. In Chapter 1, we provided some background and included demonstrations of procedures associated with the standard independent group design with two groups. In Chapter 2, we expanded this material to the case of the one-way ANOVA with $k > 2$ groups. In Chapter 3, we took the next logical step by demonstrating computational procedures for factorial ANOVA. In Chapter 4, covariates were added to the mix. In Chapter 5, various repeated measures designs were dealt with. Since our purpose was didactic in nature, examples were appropriately provided.

With that said, this monograph would be incomplete without a discussion of certain design and interpretation issues that do not fit neatly into any of the first five chapters, but are important nonetheless. These issues are dealt with in the next section.

Ancillary Issues

In presenting procedures for computing effect size values from complex ANOVA designs, several issues arise that are not critical for understanding the procedures themselves, but that deserve some attention. These issues are: (1) use of different effect size estimators in meta-analysis, (2) variability in independent variable variance across studies, (3) meta-analysis of d versus r versus test statistics, (4) unequal subgroup sizes, and (5) reporting of relevant information in published (and unpublished) work. As can be seen, these issues have to do primarily with the use of effect size values within the context of meta-analysis.

Different Effect Size Estimators

As we mentioned earlier, there exist a variety of estimators of effect size. Although Glass' d (Glass et al., 1981), Cohen's d (1969), and Hedges and Olkin's d (1985) are intended to measure the same population value δ, they contain varying degrees of bias. Hedges and Olkin's d presumably has the least bias (though not by much), but for many purposes, consistency of use of estimators is more important than eliminating the amount of bias that the Hedges and Olkin d typically eliminates. In meta-analysis, we are typically interested not only in estimating δ, but also in estimating σ_δ^2. This value is estimated by subtracting from the observed variance in effect size values the variance expected from sampling error and the variance attributable to differences in artifact values (e.g., reliability, restriction of range). If the estimate of σ_δ^2 is small, then we have support for the notion that our effect size estimate represents a single population value. However, any factor that contributes systematically to between-study differences serves to increase the observed variance in effect size values. If a meta-analysis were based on aggregation of *different* effect size estimators, then the observed variance of effect sizes would be inflated unless variability due to use of different estimators were treated as an artifact and removed from the observed variance value in the computation of σ_δ^2. This is certainly possible, but the more practical solution might be to decide on an estimator of effect size at the outset and use it throughout, thus eliminating the need to remove variability associated with the use of different estimators.

Additionally, it should be perfectly plain that these different indices will seldom yield terribly discrepant results. The distinctive feature of Glass' *d* is that the control group standard deviation, not the pooled standard deviation, serves as the denominator. Of course, the assumption of equal population variances is a common one. Thus, the control and pooled standard deviations are equal on expectation and should typically differ only by sampling error. It should be equally plain that Hedges and Olkin's *d* will differ only from the other values when sample sizes are very small. Indeed, for $N \geq 50$, *d* is seldom inflated by more than .01. Thus, for the typical study, the differences among these estimators are too small to be of great concern.

Variability in Variance of IVs

It has long been known that the amount of variance in a variable affects the extent to which it can account for variability in other variables (see Cortina & DeShon, 1998, for a discussion of these and related issues). This means that the magnitude of an effect is partly determined by the variance in the independent variable. For example, if one were to compare the average heart rate of people who smoke 15 cigarettes per day to the average heart rate of people who smoke 20 cigarettes per day and compute a *d* value, one would get a very different result than if one compared people who smoke 40 cigarettes per day to nonsmokers. The increase in independent variable variance leads to a concomitant increase in standardized mean difference.

This is not problematic, at the individual or meta-analytic study level, as long as the results are discussed in terms of the particular comparison involved. Problems can arise, however, if the variance of the particular operationalization of the IV is not explicitly recognized. Consider two examples. First, consider the two smoking studies mentioned above. There is no problem if each is discussed as a comparison of two particular groups (i.e., the group that smoked X number of cigarettes per day had an average heart rate of Y, whereas the group that smoked $X + K$ cigarettes per day had an average heart rate of $Y + J$). If, instead, the results of these studies are discussed in more general terms, (e.g., the effect of smoking on heart rate is...), then it might be concluded that these studies are in conflict with one another. In other words, because they are bound to yield different effect size values, the naive reader might conclude that they suggest different things regarding the impact of smoking when this is not necessarily the case.

Consider a meta-analytic investigation of the same relationship. Some studies use the former operationalization of smoking, and others use the latter. These studies will arrive at very different δ estimates, and the differences between these studies would affect the observed variance of the d values. The naive reader (or meta-analyst) might conclude that there are unidentified moderators of the smoking-heart rate relationship as evidenced by the estimate of σ_δ^2.

In both of these examples, the difference between the two operationalizations was the amount of variance that they produced. The population rate of change value in raw score units (i.e., the unstandardized regression weight) would presumably be the same for the two groups. That is, the expected increase in heart rate per single cigarette per day increase would be the same for both groups. However, standardized values such as d, r, and β would be expected to differ because they are partly determined by the amount of variance in the independent variable.

In those single study situations where standardized indices are desired, the only alternative is to discuss such values in terms of comparisons between specific groups as suggested above. At the meta-analytic level, an alternative solution is available. Variance of the independent variables can be treated as a moderator. This moderator can then be correlated with observed d (see p. 302 of Hunter & Schmidt, 1990, for a description of this procedure) or broken down into discrete categories. Separate estimates of δ and σ_δ^2 can then be computed for each category. Of course, each result should then be discussed in terms of comparisons between specific groups.

One final extreme groups issue stems from the "off-factors of theoretical interest" versus "off-factors not of theoretical interest" distinction. If one has an extreme groups off-factor that is not of theoretical interest, then use of the square root of the MS_{within} takes care of its influence in an appropriate fashion. However, what if the extreme groups variable is of theoretical interest? In other words, what does one do if the variable exists in the population, but with a variance that is smaller than the variance observed in the study in question? We cannot simply remove its influence by using MS_{within} because this would result in an underestimate of error. However, treating this off-factor as if it were any other off-factor of theoretical interest, perhaps by applying the N & G procedure, did not work either because the inflated variance of this off-factor caused the error estimate to be inflated as well. There are only two possible solutions to this problem. One is to try to guess what the influence of this off-factor would have been if its levels had been chosen to mimic those found in the population. This is typically not possible with any degree of accuracy. The second solution is use the N & G, Glass, or M & D procedure to compute an effect size value that generalizes only to the extreme group case. Of course, this value does not generalize to situations in which the off-factor has a different set of levels.

Neither of these solutions is especially palatable. It seems to us that the only worthwhile solution is to avoid the extreme groups design whenever standardized values such as effect size indices are desired.

Which Values Do I Meta-analyze?

The focus of this monograph has been on d values. When one is conducting a meta-analysis, however, one typically orients the analysis around d or r, but not both. Procedures for correcting either for artifacts are fairly well established, so either can be the focus of a meta-analysis. That is, regardless of the type of values presented in the primary studies involved, the meta-analysis can result in average d values or average r values. Because the correction formulas are simpler for correlations than for d values, some authors (e.g., Hunter & Schmidt, 1990; Rosenthal, 1991) have recommended that d values (and t values, F values, p values, etc.) be converted to correlations first. Meta-analytic procedures would then be applied to correlations. If one wished to discuss the results in the language of d values, then the average correlation (and all relevant distribution values) could be converted back to d values in the end.

This strikes us as a reasonable suggestion. However, we would add one note of caution. Use of correlations instead of d values does not solve any problems that exist at the primary study level. This should be obvious since r is easily converted into d and vice versa. However, some authors have suggested that conversion to r eliminates concerns with differentiating between repeated measures and independent groups designs. Dunlap et al. (1996) show that this is clearly not the case, and we refer the interested reader to Dunlap et al. for more details on this issue. There is only one reason for converting values into correlation prior to meta-analysis: simplicity.

Unequal Subgroup Sizes

Unequal sample sizes have no impact on the expected value of d. However, given a certain overall sample size, the estimate of d has less sampling error if the subgroups have equal numbers of values. In discussing the variability of d in Chapter 1, we mentioned two formulas: Equation (1.6) (Hunter & Schmidt, 1990) and Equation (1.9) (Hedges & Olkin, 1985). After showing that the two formulas yielded nearly identical values for our Example 1.1, we pointed out that the reasonably large sample size ($N = 300$) was one reason for the lack of discrepancy between these two formulas. Another reason was that there were equal numbers of values in the two subgroups. Because Equation (1.6) takes into account only the total sample size, it is insensitive to departures from equal sample size. Nevertheless, unequal sample size does have an impact on variability of d. This impact is reflected in Equation (1.9). For example, consider once again the d value yielded by Equation (1.1), .77. Suppose that the total sample size remained the same (300), but that these scores were distributed 30–270 instead of 150–150. Note that this sort of situation is not uncommon in the applied social sciences. The value from Equation (1.6) does not change, but the value from Equation (1.9) goes from .0143 to .038. The square roots of these values give us the standard error values used to construct confidence intervals. These values are .12 and .19, respectively. We do not claim that these are enormous differences. We simply wish to point out that the most commonly used formula for the variance of d, Equation (1.6), does not take unequal sample sizes into account, and such inequalities can have an impact on estimates of variability, especially for small samples.

Reporting Issues

At various points in this monograph, we have mentioned the difficulty associated with computing effect size values from published work. One reason for this difficulty is that necessary values are often not reported. With the advent of meta-analysis and increased recognition of the limitations of significance testing, reporting practices have improved. However, it is clear to anyone who has conducted a meta-analysis that things are far from perfect. In Table 6.1, we offer some reporting guidelines for research involving the ANOVA designs. Some of these guidelines are specific to particular types of designs, while others apply to most or all types of ANOVA designs.

In addition to these suggestions for the primary study, we would like to see certain systemic changes. At the very least, we would like to see journals in the social sciences require that these values be reported in all studies using ANOVA designs (and that analogous values be reported for correlational designs). In addition, the journals themselves could ensure adequate dissemination of information by maintaining a database of all data and data analytic control cards for all studies published in their pages. For most journals, this would fill the equivalent of a few 3.5″ disks per year and would ensure that any values required for subsequent reviews would be available from that point on.

TABLE 6.1

Suggested Guidelines for Reporting of Results

---

1. *All ANOVA designs—*
   a. Report *all* within-cell information including means, standard deviations, and sample sizes. Row and column information are also helpful, though not necessary.
   b. Report sums of squares and mean squares for all effects *including* nonsignificant effects.
2. *Repeated measures–correlated observations designs—*
   a. Report all values mentioned in 1. above.
   b. Report *all* measure-to-measure correlations.
3. *ANCOVA designs—*
   a. Report all values mentioned in 1. above.
   b. Report all summary statistics for all variables *including* the covariate.
   c. Report covariances (or correlations) between the dependent variable and each covariate.
   d. Report covariances (or correlations) among all covariates.

NOTES

1. The correlation between continuous variables can only be converted into a d value after at least one of the variables is artificially dichotomized. Such artificial dichotomization is typically not advisable because of the resulting loss of information.

2. This section draws heavily from Hunter and Schmidt (1990), Hedges and Olkin (1985), and Glass et al. (1981). Interested readers should consult these texts for more elaborate descriptions of this material.

3. The formula $r = .5d$ provides a reasonable approximation and functions best when $-.41 \leq d \leq .41$. Because the d value in this example is outside this interval, the formula overestimates r slightly. This simplified formula yields a correlation value of .38.

4. Of course, $t_k^2 = F_{1,k}$.

5. Thanks to an anonymous reviewer for bringing our attention to this issue.

6. Although MS_{within} is typically reported in ANOVA tables, it can also be computed directly from summary statistics in many situations. See Seifert (1991), *Educational and Psychological Measurement*, pp. 341–347.

7. There remains an issue of extreme groups designs that usually cannot be resolved statistically. This issue is addressed in the "ancillary issues" section of the monograph.

8. The M & D procedure yields only positive values, thus, it cannot be used to determine direction. This can only be done by attending to the means themselves.

9. Thanks to Bill Dunlap for pointing this out.

10. This may well be the least realistic of the examples in this monograph. Intelligence and field independence are typically found to be very highly correlated.

11. Thanks to Adam Winsler for suggesting this example.

12. See Dunlap et al. (1996) for a derivation of this formula.

13. Issues regarding extreme groups designs that were described in Chapter 3 also apply here.

APPENDIX A: AIR TRAFFIC CONTROLLER DATA SET

CONS	JOBPERF	FIELD	GENDER	TRNGVID1	RACECAT	IQ1	NUM1SP1	NUM1SP2	NUM1SP3	NUM2SP1	NUM2SP2	NUM2SP3	NUM3SP1	NUM3SP2	NUM3SP3	TRICAF	DISPCAT1
-1.228	5.886	1.00	.00	1.00	1.00	106.47	2.522	7.334	4.444	6.962	5.384	4.182	4.844	3.160	1.080	2.00	1.00
.381	7.404	1.00	.00	.00	1.00	106.62	9.342	9.386	4.794	8.870	6.848	10.230	4.104	1.700	6.214	1.00	2.00
-.470	6.810	1.00	.00	1.00	1.00	75.75	6.008	9.220	9.508	7.594	6.520	6.104	6.190	5.560	4.032	2.00	2.00
.583	12.188	1.00	.00	1.00	1.00	107.71	10.730	7.888	6.618	8.732	6.392	6.496	8.698	9.340	7.814	2.00	2.00
-.721	8.898	1.00	.00	.00	.00	116.14	5.346	6.634	6.154	2.606	6.380	3.266	.106	6.900	.360	2.00	1.00
-.780	10.446	.00	.00	1.00	2.00	108.19	5.286	8.442	4.908	6.226	6.826	5.318	4.694	9.860	5.892	2.00	2.00
-.546	6.338	1.00	.00	.00	2.00	104.67	10.378	9.976	10.352	7.128	9.654	5.616	6.348	8.520	5.966	1.00	2.00
.051	7.058	1.00	1.00	.00	1.00	111.22	6.320	8.084	9.546	5.132	9.088	10.536	5.368	8.520	5.720	2.00	1.00
.694	9.676	.00	.00	1.00	1.00	82.11	9.210	6.384	6.342	7.450	8.064	6.562	8.922	8.520	5.236	1.00	.00
1.178	7.358	.00	.00	.00	1.00	94.21	2.934	7.078	7.142	4.258	7.614	6.306	2.328	7.260	5.412	1.00	2.00
1.127	13.474	1.00	.00	1.00	1.00	123.69	6.032	7.512	8.854	5.268	6.338	12.584	6.880	7.720	5.852	2.00	1.00
-.667	11.348	.00	.00	1.00	.00	125.11	11.310	7.574	10.716	6.270	8.332	5.982	6.802	9.580	7.458	2.00	1.00
.149	10.288	1.00	.00	1.00	2.00	111.40	9.242	9.710	7.038	6.034	8.078	5.498	7.300	6.180	9.214	2.00	1.00
-1.204	7.874	.00	.00	1.00	2.00	108.48	3.622	7.364	4.922	8.148	7.858	10.802	6.250	7.220	5.340	1.00	2.00
-1.285	8.350	1.00	.00	.00	.00	87.54	11.766	9.144	9.704	11.350	10.488	4.984	8.334	7.040	5.842	2.00	2.00
-.512	9.958	1.00	.00	1.00	1.00	107.67	8.572	10.128	8.016	6.438	9.292	4.940	8.232	8.320	4.328	1.00	1.00
.689	10.338	1.00	.00	1.00	.00	117.55	8.194	10.894	9.192	8.870	8.146	10.438	8.556	9.020	10.858	1.00	.00
-1.060	7.246	1.00	.00	1.00	.00	116.30	12.232	9.622	9.730	7.902	4.386	10.202	8.378	5.840	6.786	1.00	.00
.802	6.412	.00	.00	.00	1.00	99.88	6.266	9.150	8.758	8.052	7.162	6.202	11.556	7.060	6.512	1.00	2.00
2.368	7.242	1.00	.00	1.00	.00	92.80	7.496	5.446	8.824	7.742	4.852	3.868	8.374	7.920	5.488	2.00	.00
-.707	10.890	1.00	1.00	1.00	2.00	100.54	5.248	8.048	5.670	5.368	5.196	3.022	4.458	4.620	7.234	.00	.00
.447	8.630	1.00	.00	1.00	1.00	105.45	7.258	4.814	5.408	6.400	5.978	1.548	8.470	7.760	8.666	.00	1.00
1.247	5.796	.00	.00	.00	2.00	96.63	9.552	9.552	8.496	8.326	8.298	4.046	8.208	3.660	5.172	1.00	.00
-.635	9.954	.00	1.00	1.00	.00	133.26	7.684	3.206	7.066	4.844	4.070	6.896	8.780	6.820	6.640	.00	1.00
-.700	5.982	1.00	.00	1.00	2.00	84.69	8.868	10.940	10.002	8.426	7.682	5.642	7.974	9.160	7.826	.00	.00
.907	6.972	1.00	.00	.00	.00	119.14	10.234	9.036	5.726	6.832	4.676	7.368	4.698	5.060	3.404	2.00	.00
-.197	8.122	1.00	.00	1.00	.00	117.75	11.640	7.002	2.308	7.192	8.412	3.154	8.354	4.440	2.514	1.00	2.00
-.827	5.800	1.00	.00	.00	2.00	81.73	9.752	7.324	7.822	5.930	10.648	9.432	8.498	8.120	5.884	2.00	.00
-.462	13.014	1.00	.00	1.00	1.00	118.86	8.376	9.850	7.912	8.958	5.610	6.206	8.148	7.380	6.538	2.00	.00
.629	7.332	1.00	1.00	1.00	.00	118.81	9.150	10.428	7.046	7.088	10.940	9.184	7.314	7.440	7.024	1.00	1.00
-.206	7.040	.00	.00	.00	.00	99.96	7.106	7.624	4.150	10.692	9.654	6.366	9.458	6.080	7.224	.00	.00
-.721	8.582	1.00	.00	1.00	2.00	132.70	7.180	10.826	8.506	9.968	12.442	6.538	7.150	10.460	4.376	1.00	1.00
-.306	10.458	1.00	.00	.00	1.00	91.84	5.306	8.072	4.150	9.656	8.226	6.586	8.634	4.800	5.562	2.00	2.00
-.216	7.198	.00	.00	1.00	1.00	91.39	9.880	4.370	5.262	7.394	5.074	5.894	5.918	6.100	4.922	2.00	.00
.713	13.318	.00	.00	1.00	2.00	126.64	9.960	8.498	4.218	7.088	7.400	7.166	6.466	9.260	4.282	2.00	.00
-.704	4.956	.00	.00	.00	2.00	100.54	6.114	7.534	7.562	8.994	8.948	6.824	2.832	6.560	5.186	2.00	.00
-1.538	7.050	.00	.00	1.00	1.00	58.99	6.710	9.804	8.490	1.936	8.948	8.258	6.254	9.040	3.596	.00	.00
-1.867	6.452	.00	1.00	.00	2.00	120.30	5.696	4.996	6.326	4.422	6.242	8.164	5.412	6.760	5.966	2.00	2.00
-2.009	5.758	.00	1.00	.00	.00	114.21	5.874	5.526	6.310	3.990	6.908	7.704	7.902	7.660	6.380	2.00	.00
1.976	8.066	.00	.00	1.00	.00	93.01	7.434	6.608	6.232	7.212	9.778	3.996	5.758	7.160	1.894	2.00	2.00
-1.056	12.004	.00	.00	.00	.00	89.13	9.334	8.320	6.076	7.286	5.100	7.154	3.950	8.780	7.744	1.00	1.00
.044	10.228	1.00	1.00	1.00	.00	103.06	9.554	8.842	6.238	5.614	5.384	4.480	3.950	10.440	5.382	1.00	1.00
1.317	10.228	1.00	1.00	1.00	.00	120.52	10.500	8.328	7.752	10.134	7.402	7.148	9.976	6.900	6.280	2.00	2.00

-.723	7.130	1.08	.00	80.73	9.390	6.848	5.004	6.754	7.474	4.520	6.480	9.260	5.594	.00	1.00	1.00
-.859	9.674	.00	1.00	100.68	5.214	10.016	5.748	5.128	8.078	6.622	4.320	2.860	6.370	1.00	1.00	2.00
-.487	10.536	1.00	1.00	105.36	2.550	2.550	7.206	6.510	6.102	6.388	6.800	6.800	3.792	2.00	2.00	2.00
.271	8.554	.00	2.00	80.35	10.278	6.782	7.964	6.760	6.102	6.388	9.074	6.540	8.356	1.00	1.00	.00
-.625	5.888	.00	2.00	91.18	7.700	9.316	7.000	6.434	6.646	6.872	5.748	10.580	3.120	2.00	2.00	2.00
.950	10.690	1.00	.00	110.89	6.798	6.694	2.804	8.610	7.430	9.762	9.174	7.560	7.672	1.00	1.00	1.00
1.504	10.912	1.00	2.00	109.74	4.888	8.740	6.658	6.544	5.794	5.546	7.954	5.560	4.660	2.00	.00	.00
.721	5.204	.00	1.00	94.12	7.482	6.134	7.706	5.960	5.674	8.490	6.618	5.560	5.048	1.00	1.00	1.00
2.411	8.946	1.00	1.00	123.40	4.494	6.314	7.880	7.904	5.704	7.540	7.066	8.580	9.746	1.00	1.00	1.00
.840	4.432	.00	2.00	97.32	9.344	8.514	6.980	5.960	5.674	5.674	6.622	5.640	3.050	2.00	2.00	1.00
-1.356	7.774	.00	2.00	76.99	8.292	6.058	8.658	6.512	5.916	4.494	4.608	5.400	5.314	2.00	.00	1.00
-.970	10.678	1.00	1.00	111.09	8.720	8.042	5.990	7.556	5.926	4.220	6.272	5.400	7.998	1.00	2.00	1.00
-.330	9.442	1.00	2.00	108.85	8.710	8.426	6.802	10.248	5.448	7.252	7.222	10.740	7.704	1.00	.00	2.00
-2.043	10.106	.00	.00	105.64	8.478	10.490	6.852	8.854	6.506	4.678	7.352	9.040	6.938	2.00	1.00	.00
-.937	6.190	1.00	1.00	85.16	7.366	8.124	9.210	7.464	6.244	4.556	7.776	6.480	3.720	.00	1.00	.00
-1.467	6.456	1.00	1.00	88.98	6.660	6.034	8.012	4.424	4.654	6.102	7.880	6.000	4.864	2.00	.00	2.00
.054	9.326	.00	.00	95.76	6.516	6.116	8.484	6.528	5.834	5.580	9.328	7.920	7.732	.00	2.00	.00
-.313	6.098	1.00	.00	120.76	5.910	5.978	8.062	9.802	5.242	5.546	9.332	8.000	3.174	1.00	.00	1.00
-.928	5.608	.00	.00	97.65	4.338	7.386	6.980	3.796	6.332	1.524	4.298	2.960	7.198	1.00	1.00	2.00
-.357	6.604	1.00	2.00	90.39	11.396	8.034	9.320	9.008	11.222	7.614	7.520	7.520	6.686	.00	1.00	2.00
-.288	7.618	.00	1.00	110.47	7.032	9.162	9.248	8.744	7.182	7.888	8.394	6.680	6.264	1.00	2.00	.00
-.384	3.438	1.00	2.00	77.13	8.090	10.892	10.802	8.468	6.844	5.530	5.522	7.100	9.634	2.00	.00	1.00
.129	6.099	1.00	1.00	91.27	12.028	10.892	10.396	8.210	7.562	7.392	10.100	7.324	5.904	.00	1.00	.00
-.259	5.838	.00	1.00	68.28	9.872	10.080	4.158	6.764	9.558	3.442	7.996	8.330	8.318	2.00	1.00	1.00
-.210	10.078	1.00	2.00	102.19	7.864	6.922	8.058	8.084	6.844	3.818	8.074	6.340	7.100	.00	.00	.00
-.788	8.704	.00	1.00	96.93	6.688	9.692	7.226	6.288	6.084	7.392	7.324	5.350	5.494	1.00	1.00	.00
.104	6.034	1.00	.00	90.24	10.150	7.832	10.082	5.778	4.812	3.442	3.998	5.480	5.870	.00	1.00	1.00
.917	7.484	.00	1.00	101.22	9.348	6.886	6.864	8.990	9.094	7.586	4.206	7.260	6.970	1.00	.00	.00
-.171	6.638	1.00	.00	109.21	9.786	8.806	10.796	4.810	6.294	9.094	7.976	4.500	7.344	.00	2.00	2.00
.109	8.196	1.00	1.00	118.96	8.006	3.998	6.244	9.494	6.978	2.622	7.012	4.260	5.422	1.00	2.00	2.00
.076	8.824	.00	2.00	93.96	8.660	7.892	7.266	6.774	6.880	3.818	4.694	7.760	2.370	2.00	1.00	1.00
1.038	9.500	1.00	2.00	143.79	10.334	7.274	7.860	5.292	6.978	6.196	6.934	5.380	2.370	2.00	1.00	1.00
-1.497	4.806	.00	2.00	82.59	8.220	8.220	5.756	5.292	7.332	4.206	3.998	5.600	7.096	.00	.00	2.00
-.336	6.254	1.00	2.00	127.02	6.350	10.328	8.832	9.560	8.048	8.496	7.924	4.500	3.732	.00	.00	2.00
-1.465	9.720	1.00	.00	100.62	7.140	5.694	4.930	7.076	9.158	7.012	7.400	6.516	.00	.00	1.00	1.00
1.957	10.050	.00	1.00	106.99	7.458	6.558	2.512	7.854	7.904	4.554	1.184	4.980	3.662	1.00	1.00	2.00
.117	10.982	.00	1.00	92.17	10.792	7.984	5.178	5.268	5.488	3.892	6.640	4.184	3.684	.00	2.00	2.00
.578	11.588	.00	2.00	105.93	7.794	6.300	8.932	9.892	9.516	9.094	7.996	7.260	4.108	2.00	2.00	.00
3.613	7.838	1.00	2.00	113.92	5.620	7.028	5.718	5.718	5.762	4.620	6.926	7.000	4.512	1.00	1.00	1.00
.609	9.816	.00	1.00	103.95	6.122	6.558	6.956	6.368	6.062	4.254	5.090	5.860	3.362	.00	.00	2.00
-3.275	9.878	.00	2.00	103.51	11.906	8.466	8.872	8.872	6.382	9.970	8.268	6.680	5.092	2.00	1.00	2.00
-.153	5.768	1.00	1.00	99.63	5.620	8.654	7.794	8.770	7.370	5.554	8.616	4.780	7.336	1.00	1.00	2.00
-.261	8.710	1.00	1.00	129.79	6.880	6.744	3.818	6.286	7.728	6.134	5.974	6.580	4.430	.00	1.00	1.00
.677	8.724	1.00	1.00	129.79	6.720	10.414	8.454	6.790	8.918	5.554	6.440	5.360	6.586	1.00	2.00	2.00

APPENDIX A: AIR TRAFFIC CONTROLLER DATA SET (Continued)

-.164	8.546	1.00	1.00	1.00	.00	93.33	5.840	5.070	6.996	3.570	6.076	7.170	5.766	8.220	4.262	.00	2.00
.676	7.896	1.00	.00	1.00	2.00	134.49	7.066	8.290	7.200	9.810	6.980	6.694	5.174	6.660	7.992	2.00	2.00
-.434	5.912	1.00	.00	1.00	1.00	100.69	7.222	6.236	5.062	5.988	5.274	3.122	3.640	2.280		.00	2.00
-.225	6.780	.00	.00	2.00	2.00	113.62	8.068	9.584	8.672	7.626	6.834	5.154	1.896	5.940	7.966	.00	.00
-.551	5.832	1.00	1.00	1.00	1.00	72.01	8.390	5.886	5.858	3.734	5.336	2.882	8.330	8.460	3.890	.00	1.00
-.651	9.620	1.00	1.00	1.00	1.00	82.51	6.816	6.802	5.924	8.554	1.140	3.300	5.994	5.440	4.838	2.00	
-1.645	3.796	.00	.00	1.00	2.00	69.64	9.474	8.452	11.586	8.276	6.104	8.406	4.804	7.020	8.340	.00	.00
.398	7.580	.00	1.00	1.00	1.00	116.49	9.858	8.872	7.816	6.360	1.928	7.466	7.338	2.520	4.542	1.00	2.00
-.159	11.742	.00	1.00	1.00	1.00	102.18	6.822	7.132	8.120	10.018	7.956	8.360	8.528	6.020	8.942	.00	2.00
1.091	10.360	.00	1.00	1.00	2.00	119.82	4.400	1.058	1.572	3.208	2.714	2.892	3.460	2.800	2.984	.00	.00
-.420	8.536	1.00	1.00	2.00	1.00	104.76	7.126	8.538	7.408	6.854	5.922	8.594	8.278	7.800	4.510	.00	.00
.665	7.614	1.00	1.00	1.00	1.00	117.12	7.188	5.242	7.058	7.934	4.956	4.876	6.256	9.960	6.250	.00	1.00
.754	5.490	.00	1.00	1.00	1.00	111.25	11.310	7.574	10.716	6.270	8.332	5.982	6.802	9.580	7.458	1.00	1.00
-1.228	5.886	1.00	1.00	1.00	1.00	106.47	2.522	7.334	4.444	6.962	5.384	4.182	4.844	3.160	1.080	2.00	2.00
.381	7.404	.00	.00	1.00	1.00	75.75	9.342	9.386	4.794	8.870	8.848	10.230	4.104	4.700	6.214	1.00	1.00
-.470	6.810	.00	1.00	1.00	1.00	107.71	6.008	9.220	9.508	7.594	6.520	6.104	6.190	5.560	4.032	2.00	2.00
-.583	12.188	1.00	.00	1.00	2.00	116.14	10.730	7.888	6.618	8.732	6.392	6.496	6.688	9.340	7.814	2.00	1.00
-.721	8.898	1.00	.00	1.00	1.00	111.22	5.346	6.634	6.154	2.606	6.380	3.266	.106	6.900	.360	1.00	2.00
-.780	10.446	.00	.00	1.00	2.00	108.19	5.286	8.442	4.908	6.226	6.826	5.318	4.694	9.860	5.892	2.00	2.00
-.546	6.338	1.00	1.00	1.00	2.00	104.67	10.378	9.976	10.352	7.128	9.654	5.616	6.348	8.520	5.966	2.00	1.00
.051	7.058	1.00	1.00	1.00	1.00	111.40	11.310	7.574	9.546	5.132	9.088	10.536	5.368	3.480	5.720	1.00	2.00
.694	9.676	.00	.00	1.00	1.00	82.11	9.210	6.384	6.342	7.450	8.064	6.562	8.922	8.520	5.236	2.00	1.00
1.178	7.358	1.00	.00	1.00	2.00	94.21	2.934	7.078	7.142	4.258	7.614	6.306	2.328	5.260	5.412	1.00	2.00
1.127	13.474	1.00	.00	1.00	1.00	123.69	6.032	7.512	8.854	5.268	6.338	12.584	6.880	7.720	5.852	2.00	1.00
-.667	11.348	1.00	1.00	1.00	2.00	125.11	11.310	7.574	10.716	6.270	8.332	5.982	6.802	9.580	7.458	1.00	.00
-.149	10.288	1.00	1.00	1.00	.00	111.40	11.440	7.038	7.038	6.034	8.078	5.498	6.180	9.224	9.224	1.00	.00
-1.204	7.874	.00	.00	1.00	2.00	100.48	3.622	7.364	4.922	8.148	7.858	10.802	6.250	7.220	5.340	1.00	2.00
-1.285	7.242	.00	.00	1.00	1.00	87.54	11.766	9.144	9.704	4.258	11.350	10.488	4.984	7.040	5.842	2.00	2.00
-.512	9.958	1.00	.00	1.00	1.00	107.67	8.572	10.128	8.016	6.438	9.292	4.940	8.232	8.320	4.328	1.00	1.00
.689	10.338	1.00	.00	1.00	.00	117.55	8.194	10.894	9.192	8.870	8.146	10.438	8.556	9.020	10.858	1.00	.00
-1.060	7.246	1.00	.00	1.00	.00	106.30	12.232	9.622	9.730	7.902	4.386	10.202	8.378	5.840	6.786	1.00	.00
.802	6.412	.00	.00	1.00	.00	98.88	8.868	9.150	8.758	8.052	7.362	6.202	11.556	7.060	6.512	1.00	.00
2.368	7.242	.00	.00	1.00	.00	92.80	7.496	5.446	8.824	7.742	4.852	3.868	8.374	7.920	5.488	2.00	2.00
-.707	10.890	1.00	.00	1.00	.00	100.54	5.248	6.048	5.670	5.368	5.196	3.022	4.458	4.620	7.234	.00	1.00
.447	8.630	1.00	.00	1.00	1.00	105.45	7.258	4.814	5.408	6.400	5.978	1.548	8.470	7.760	8.666	.00	.00
1.247	5.796	2.00	.00	1.00	2.00	96.63	9.552	8.496	8.326	4.928	4.298	4.046	8.208	3.660	5.172	1.00	1.00
-.635	9.954	2.00	.00	1.00	.00	133.26	7.684	7.066	10.002	4.844	4.070	6.896	8.780	6.820	6.640	.00	.00
-.700	6.972	2.00	.00	1.00	.00	84.69	8.868	8.868	10.940	8.426	7.682	5.642	7.974	9.160	7.826	2.00	1.00
.907	6.972	.00	.00	1.00	.00	119.14	10.234	9.036	5.726	6.832	4.676	7.368	4.698	5.060	3.404	2.00	.00
-.197	8.122	.00	.00	2.00	.00	117.75	11.640	7.002	2.308	7.192	8.412	3.154	8.354	4.440	2.514	1.00	2.00
-.827	5.800	.00	.00	1.00	.00	81.73	9.752	7.324	7.822	5.930	10.648	9.432	8.498	8.120	5.884	2.00	2.00
-.462	13.014	1.00	.00	1.00	1.00	120.86	9.850	7.912	5.930	8.958	5.610	6.206	8.148	7.380	6.538	2.00	1.00
.629	7.332	1.00	.00	1.00	2.00	118.81	9.150	7.046	7.088	7.088	10.940	9.184	7.314	7.440	7.024	1.00	2.00
-.206	7.040	1.00	1.00	1.00	.00	99.96	7.106	7.624	4.150	10.692	9.654	9.366	9.458	6.080	7.224	.00	.00

1.00	.00	4.376	10.460	7.150	6.538	12.442	9.968	8.506	10.072	7.180	132.70	.00	1.00	.00	1.00	8.582	-.721
2.00	2.00	5.562	4.300	7.634	6.586	8.226	7.394	9.656	8.072	5.306	91.84	2.00	.00	.00	1.00	10.458	-.306
.00	2.00	4.922	6.100	5.894	6.934	6.934	5.074	5.262	4.370	9.880	93.39	1.00	.00	.00	1.00	7.198	-.216
1.00	1.00	4.282	9.260	6.466	7.166	7.400	7.088	7.420	8.498	9.960	126.64	.00	.00	.00	1.00	11.318	.713
.00	.00	5.186	6.560	6.254	6.824	8.948	7.562	8.490	7.534	6.114	100.54	.00	1.00	.00	1.00	4.956	-.704
.00	2.00	3.596	9.040	6.412	8.258	8.258	1.936	6.326	4.996	6.710	58.99	1.00	.00	.00	1.00	7.050	-1.538
2.00	2.00	5.966	6.760	7.902	8.164	6.242	4.422	6.310	5.526	5.696	120.30	.00	.00	1.00	1.00	4.498	-1.867
2.00	1.00	6.380	7.660	7.758	7.704	6.908	7.212	6.232	5.608	5.674	114.21	.00	1.00	1.00	1.00	6.452	-2.008
.00	1.00	1.894	7.160	3.950	3.996	9.778	7.286	6.076	6.608	5.434	93.01	1.00	.00	.00	1.00	5.758	1.976
.00	2.00	7.744	8.780	5.812	7.100	5.384	5.614	6.238	6.320	9.334	89.13	.00	1.00	.00	1.00	8.066	-1.056
1.00	1.00	5.382	10.440	9.976	4.480	5.384	7.286	6.076	8.842	9.554	103.06	.00	.00	1.00	1.00	12.004	.044
2.00	2.00	6.280	6.900	4.320	7.148	7.474	6.754	7.752	8.328	6.848	120.52	2.00	.00	.00	1.00	10.228	1.317
1.00	1.00	5.594	9.260	9.074	4.520	8.078	5.128	5.004	6.848	9.390	80.73	1.00	.00	.00	1.00	7.110	-.723
2.00	1.00	6.370	2.860	5.748	6.622	8.078	6.754	5.748	10.016	5.214	100.68	.00	1.00	.00	1.00	9.674	-.859
.00	.00	3.792	6.800	8.990	6.326	7.474	7.968	5.748	2.550	5.002	105.36	1.00	.00	.00	1.00	10.536	-.487
.00	1.00	8.356	6.640	7.954	6.388	6.102	6.510	7.206	6.782	10.278	80.35	.00	1.00	.00	1.00	8.554	.271
1.00	2.00	3.320	10.580	9.174	7.688	3.866	6.760	7.964	9.316	7.700	91.18	.00	.00	1.00	1.00	5.888	-.625
2.00	2.00	7.672	8.980	7.066	6.872	7.688	6.434	6.964	6.694	6.798	110.89	.00	1.00	.00	1.00	10.690	.950
2.00	1.00	4.660	7.560	6.622	9.762	7.430	8.610	2.804	7.000	4.888	109.74	.00	.00	.00	1.00	10.912	1.504
1.00	1.00	5.048	6.560	4.608	9.174	6.704	7.304	6.658	6.740	7.432	94.12	1.00	.00	.00	1.00	5.204	.721
.00	1.00	7.724	8.580	6.272	7.540	5.674	5.960	7.880	8.314	4.494	123.40	.00	1.00	.00	1.00	8.946	2.411
1.00	2.00	9.746	5.640	7.222	6.494	5.916	6.544	7.706	6.134	3.344	97.32	.00	.00	.00	1.00	4.432	.840
1.00	1.00	5.314	5.400	7.352	4.220	5.926	6.512	8.658	6.058	8.292	76.99	.00	1.00	.00	1.00	7.774	-1.356
1.00	2.00	7.998	10.740	7.222	7.252	9.448	7.556	8.658	8.042	8.720	111.09	.00	.00	1.00	1.00	10.678	-.970
.00	1.00	7.704	9.040	7.776	4.678	10.248	10.248	5.990	8.490	8.710	108.85	.00	1.00	.00	1.00	9.442	.330
2.00	2.00	6.938	3.480	7.776	4.556	8.854	8.854	6.852	8.426	8.478	105.64	.00	.00	.00	1.00	10.106	-2.043
.00	.00	3.720	3.720	9.328	4.678	4.244	7.464	9.210	8.426	7.366	85.36	.00	1.00	.00	1.00	6.190	.937
1.00	2.00	4.864	7.920	9.332	4.556	4.244	7.464	8.012	6.834	6.660	88.98	.00	.00	.00	1.00	6.456	-1.467
2.00	1.00	3.174	8.000	4.298	5.580	5.834	6.528	8.484	6.116	10.516	95.76	.00	1.00	.00	1.00	9.326	-.054
1.00	.00	7.198	2.960	1.524	5.242	7.610	9.802	8.062	5.978	5.910	120.76	.00	.00	.00	1.00	6.098	-.313
.00	.00	6.686	7.520	8.394	1.524	11.222	9.008	9.920	6.980	7.386	97.65	.00	1.00	.00	1.00	5.608	.928
1.00	1.00	9.634	7.880	5.522	7.614	7.182	9.248	9.248	10.424	11.396	90.39	.00	.00	.00	1.00	6.604	-.357
2.00	2.00	7.732	6.680	2.836	8.134	7.182	8.468	10.802	8.034	7.032	110.47	.00	1.00	.00	1.00	7.618	-.288
1.00	1.00	5.904	6.220	10.100	7.562	7.756	8.210	10.396	10.892	7.864	77.13	.00	1.00	.00	1.00	3.438	.384
2.00	.00	8.318	6.380	8.074	8.058	6.844	8.084	8.058	10.892	9.872	68.28	.00	.00	1.00	1.00	11.600	.129
2.00	.00	5.494	6.340	7.124	7.324	4.812	5.778	7.226	10.082	7.864	122.19	.00	1.00	.00	1.00	5.838	-.259
1.00	.00	5.870	7.100	7.100	6.084	9.094	8.744	6.288	9.692	6.688	96.93	.00	.00	.00	1.00	8.704	-.210
1.00	1.00	6.970	6.360	7.586	7.392	2.622	8.930	6.886	7.832	9.348	90.24	.00	1.00	.00	1.00	6.034	-.788
1.00	2.00	7.344	6.480	9.392	4.040	4.812	4.810	6.864	9.162	101.21	109.21	.00	.00	.00	1.00	6.638	-.104
.00	2.00	5.422	8.560	7.694	7.586	4.884	9.494	10.796	9.348	118.96	.00	1.00	.00	1.00	8.196	-.917
1.00	2.00	4.678	4.260	7.694	9.392	1.818	7.860	7.266	9.786	93.96	.00	.00	.00	1.00	6.824	-.171
1.00	2.00	2.370	5.380	6.934	6.196	6.978	5.292	6.068	7.274	143.79	2.00	.00	1.00	1.00	9.500	1.038

APPENDIX A: AIR TRAFFIC CONTROLLER DATA SET (Continued)

-1.497	.00	1.00	.00	4.806	1.00	.00	2.00	2.00	82.59	9.800	8.220	5.756	6.292	7.332	4.206	3.998	6.600	7.096	1.00	1.00	1.00
-.336	1.00	.00	.00	6.254	1.00	2.00	.00	2.00	127.02	6.350	10.328	8.832	9.560	8.048	8.496	7.976	4.500	3.712	1.00	.00	.00
-1.465	1.00	1.00	1.00	9.720	1.00	.00	.00	.00	100.62	7.140	5.694	4.930	7.076	9.158	7.012	10.946	7.400	6.516	1.00	2.00	1.00
1.957	.00	.00	1.00	10.982	1.00	.00	.00	1.00	106.99	7.458	7.984	2.512	7.854	7.904	4.554	4.184	6.640	3.662	.00	1.00	.00
.117	1.00	.00	.00	10.050	.00	.00	1.00	1.00	92.17	10.792	6.558	5.178	5.268	6.488	3.892	6.690	4.980	3.684	2.00	2.00	.00
.578	1.00	.00	.00	11.588	1.00	.00	.00	.00	105.93	7.794	6.300	8.922	9.892	9.516	7.924	7.996	7.260	4.108	.00	.00	.00
3.613	.00	1.00	.00	7.838	1.00	2.00	.00	2.00	113.92	5.620	7.828	5.718	8.670	5.762	4.620	6.926	7.000	4.512	1.00	.00	2.00
.609	1.00	1.00	1.00	9.816	1.00	.00	.00	2.00	103.95	6.122	8.466	6.956	6.368	6.062	4.254	5.090	5.860	3.362	.00	2.00	.00
-3.275	1.00	.00	.00	5.768	1.00	2.00	.00	1.00	103.51	13.690	8.654	8.072	7.370	7.262	7.704	8.268	6.680	5.092	1.00	1.00	2.00
-.153	1.00	.00	.00	9.878	1.00	.00	.00	2.00	99.34	11.906	10.986	7.794	8.770	8.382	9.970	8.616	5.860	7.336	1.00	.00	2.00
-.261	1.00	.00	.00	8.710	1.00	.00	.00	2.00	99.63	6.880	6.744	3.818	8.286	7.720	6.134	5.974	4.780	4.430	.00	2.00	1.00
.677	1.00	1.00	.00	8.724	1.00	.00	.00	1.00	129.79	6.720	10.414	8.454	6.790	8.918	6.554	5.554	5.360	6.586	2.00	1.00	2.00
-.364	1.00	1.00	1.00	8.546	.00	.00	.00	.00	93.33	5.840	5.070	6.996	3.570	6.076	7.170	5.766	8.220	4.262	2.00	2.00	.00
.676	1.00	.00	.00	7.896	2.00	.00	.00	2.00	134.49	7.066	8.290	7.200	9.810	6.980	6.694	5.174	6.660	7.992	1.00	2.00	2.00
-.434	1.00	.00	.00	5.912	1.00	.00	.00	2.00	100.69	7.222	6.236	5.062	5.388	7.902	5.274	3.122	3.640	2.280	2.00	.00	2.00
-.225	.00	.00	.00	6.780	2.00	.00	.00	2.00	113.62	8.068	9.584	8.672	7.626	6.834	5.154	6.896	5.940	7.966	.00	.00	.00
-.551	1.00	1.00	.00	5.832	1.00	.00	.00	1.00	72.01	8.390	5.886	5.858	5.336	2.882	8.330	8.460	6.990	3.890	.00	.00	1.00
-.651	1.00	1.00	1.00	9.620	2.00	.00	.00	2.00	82.51	5.816	6.802	5.924	3.734	1.140	3.300	5.994	5.440	4.038	2.00	2.00	.00
-1.645	1.00	.00	.00	3.796	2.00	.00	.00	.00	69.64	9.474	8.452	11.586	8.276	6.104	8.406	4.804	7.020	8.340	.00	.00	.00
-.398	1.00	1.00	1.00	7.580	.00	.00	.00	.00	116.49	9.858	8.872	7.816	6.360	1.928	7.466	7.338	2.520	4.542	1.00	1.00	2.00
-.159	.00	1.00	.00	11.742	1.00	.00	.00	2.00	102.18	6.822	7.132	8.120	10.018	7.956	8.360	8.528	6.020	8.942	.00	.00	.00
1.091	.00	.00	.00	10.360	1.00	.00	.00	.00	119.82	4.400	1.058	1.572	3.208	2.714	2.892	3.460	2.800	2.984	.00	.00	.00
-.420	1.00	1.00	1.00	8.536	1.00	.00	.00	1.00	104.76	7.126	8.538	7.408	6.854	5.922	8.594	8.278	7.800	4.510	.00	2.00	.00
-.665	1.00	.00	.00	7.614	1.00	.00	.00	.00	117.12	7.188	5.242	7.058	7.934	4.956	4.876	8.256	9.960	6.250	.00	.00	.00
-.754	1.00	.00	.00	9.490	1.00	.00	.00	.00	111.25	11.310	7.574	10.716	6.270	8.332	5.982	6.802	9.580	7.458	1.00	1.00	1.00
-1.228	1.00	.00	.00	5.886	1.00	.00	.00	1.00	106.47	2.522	7.334	4.444	6.962	5.304	4.182	6.844	3.160	1.080	1.00	2.00	1.00
-.381	1.00	.00	.00	7.404	1.00	.00	.00	1.00	106.62	9.342	9.386	4.794	8.870	6.848	10.230	4.104	4.700	6.214	.00	1.00	2.00
-.470	1.00	.00	.00	6.810	1.00	.00	.00	1.00	75.75	6.008	9.220	9.508	7.594	6.520	6.104	6.190	5.560	4.032	.00	2.00	2.00
-.583	1.00	.00	.00	12.188	1.00	.00	.00	1.00	107.71	10.730	7.888	6.618	8.732	6.392	6.496	8.688	9.340	7.814	.00	2.00	2.00
-.721	1.00	.00	.00	8.898	1.00	.00	.00	1.00	116.14	5.346	6.634	6.154	2.606	6.380	3.266	.106	6.900	.360	.00	2.00	2.00
-.780	.00	.00	.00	10.446	1.00	.00	.00	2.00	108.19	5.286	8.442	4.908	6.226	6.826	5.318	4.694	9.860	5.892	.00	2.00	2.00
-.546	1.00	.00	.00	6.338	1.00	.00	.00	2.00	104.67	10.378	9.976	10.352	7.128	9.654	5.616	6.348	8.520	5.966	.00	2.00	2.00
.051	1.00	1.00	.00	7.058	1.00	.00	.00	1.00	111.22	6.320	8.084	9.546	5.112	9.088	10.536	5.368	3.480	5.720	1.00	2.00	1.00
.694	1.00	.00	.00	9.676	1.00	.00	.00	1.00	82.11	9.210	6.384	6.342	7.450	8.064	10.536	5.368	3.480	5.720	.00	1.00	1.00
1.178	1.00	.00	.00	7.358	1.00	.00	.00	1.00	94.21	2.934	7.078	7.142	4.258	7.614	6.306	2.328	5.260	5.412	2.00	1.00	2.00
1.127	1.00	.00	.00	13.474	1.00	.00	.00	1.00	123.69	6.032	7.512	8.854	5.268	6.338	12.584	6.880	5.260	5.852	1.00	1.00	2.00
-.667	1.00	.00	.00	11.348	1.00	.00	.00	.00	125.11	11.310	10.716	10.716	6.270	8.332	5.982	6.802	7.720	7.458	2.00	2.00	1.00
-.149	1.00	.00	1.00	10.288	2.00	.00	.00	2.00	111.40	9.242	9.710	7.038	6.034	8.078	5.498	7.300	6.180	9.214	2.00	1.00	2.00
-1.204	.00	.00	1.00	7.874	2.00	.00	.00	2.00	108.48	3.622	7.364	4.922	8.148	7.858	10.802	6.250	7.220	5.340	.00	2.00	1.00
-1.285	.00	1.00	.00	8.350	1.00	.00	.00	2.00	87.54	11.766	9.144	9.704	11.350	8.148	8.334	6.250	7.040	5.842	.00	1.00	2.00
-.512	1.00	1.00	1.00	9.958	1.00	.00	.00	1.00	107.67	8.572	10.128	8.016	6.438	9.292	4.940	8.232	8.320	4.328	1.00	1.00	2.00
.689	.00	.00	.00	10.338	1.00	.00	.00	.00	117.55	8.194	10.894	9.192	8.870	8.146	10.438	8.556	9.020	10.858	1.00	1.00	1.00
-1.060	1.00	1.00	1.00	7.246	1.00	.00	.00	.00	106.30	12.232	9.622	9.730	7.902	4.386	10.202	4.386	5.840	6.786	1.00	1.00	1.00
.802	1.00	.00	1.00	6.412	1.00	.00	.00	1.00	98.88	6.266	9.150	8.758	8.052	7.362	6.202	11.556	5.840	6.512	1.00	1.00	1.00

```
 .00   .00   2.00  5.488  7.920  8.374  3.068  4.852  7.742  8.824  5.446  7.496  92.80  1.00  .00  .00  .00  7.242  .00  2.368
 .00   .00   .00   7.234  4.620  4.458  3.022  5.196  5.368  5.670  8.048  5.248  100.54 2.00 1.00 1.00 1.00 10.890 1.00 -.707
1.00  1.00   1.00  8.666  7.760  8.208  1.548  5.978  6.400  5.408  4.814  7.258  105.45 1.00  .00  .00  .00  8.630  .00  .447
 .00   .00   1.00  5.172  6.820  8.780  4.046  8.298  4.928  8.326  8.496  9.552  96.63  2.00 1.00 1.00 1.00 5.796  1.00 1.247
1.00   .00   .00   6.640  6.820  8.780  4.070  4.070  4.844  7.066  3.206  7.684  133.26 2.00 1.00 1.00 1.00 9.954  .00 -.635
 .00   .00   .00   7.826  9.160  7.974  5.642  4.676  8.426  10.002 10.940 8.868  84.69  .00  .00  .00  1.00 5.982  .00 -.700
 .00  2.00   .00   3.404  5.050  7.698  7.368  8.412  6.832  5.726  9.036  10.234 119.14 .00  .00  .00  .00  6.972  .00 -.907
 .00   .00  2.00   2.514  4.440  8.154  3.154  8.412  7.192  2.308  7.002  11.640 117.75 .00 1.00 1.00 1.00 8.122  .00 -.197
2.00  1.00   .00   5.084  8.120  8.498  9.432  10.648 5.930  7.822  7.324  9.752  81.73  2.00 1.00 1.00 1.00 5.800  .00 -.827
1.00  2.00  1.00   6.538  7.330  8.148  6.206  5.610  8.958  7.912  9.850  8.376  128.86 .00 1.00 1.00 1.00 13.014 1.00 -.462
1.00   .00  1.00   7.024  7.440  7.314  9.184  10.940 7.088  7.046  10.428 9.150  118.81 2.00 1.00 1.00 1.00 7.332  1.00 .629
1.00  1.00   .00   7.224  6.080  9.458  6.366  9.654  10.692 4.150  7.624  7.106  99.96  .00 1.00 1.00 1.00 7.040  .00 -.206
 .00  2.00  2.00   4.376  10.460 8.634  6.586  6.538  9.568  8.506  10.826 7.180  132.70 1.00 .00 .00 1.00 8.582  1.00 -.721
2.00   .00  1.00   5.562  4.800  5.918  6.586  12.442 9.568  8.506  10.826 7.180  91.84  .00 .00 .00 .00 10.458 .00 -.306
 .00  1.00   .00   4.922  6.100  8.258  5.094  6.934  5.074  5.262  4.370  5.306  91.39  1.00 .00 .00 .00 7.198  .00 -.216
1.00   .00  1.00   4.282  9.260  5.412  6.466  6.254  1.936  6.310  6.608  5.874  126.64 .00 .00 .00 .00 13.318 .00 .713
 .00  2.00   .00   5.186  6.560  7.902  5.894  5.758  7.088  7.420  8.498  9.880  100.54 2.00 .00 .00 1.00 4.956  .00 -.704
2.00  1.00  2.00   5.966  6.760  2.832  6.824  8.948  7.562  6.076  7.533  9.960  58.99  1.00 .00 .00 1.00 12.004 .00 -1.538
 .00   .00  1.00   6.380  7.660  8.258  8.164  6.242  1.936  6.238  8.842  6.114  103.06 1.00 .00 .00 1.00 7.050  .00 -1.317
2.00  2.00  2.00   1.894  7.160  3.950  8.164  3.990  4.422  7.752  8.328  6.710  120.52 2.00 .00 .00 .00 10.228 1.00 -1.723
 .00   .00   .00   5.966  5.740  8.258  3.996  9.778  7.212  6.326  6.848  5.696  120.30 2.00 .00 .00 .00 7.130  .00 -.859
1.00  2.00  2.00   7.744  9.260  9.976  7.154  5.100  7.286  6.310  5.526  5.874  114.21 .00 .00 .00 1.00 9.674  .00 -.487
2.00   .00  1.00   5.382  6.780  5.812  4.480  5.384  5.614  6.076  4.996  8.320  93.01  .00 .00 1.00 .00 10.536 1.00 -.271
1.00  1.00  2.00   6.280  10.440 9.976  7.148  5.384  4.384  6.238  8.842  9.334  89.13  .00 .00 1.00 .00 8.554  .00 -.625
 .00  1.00  1.00   5.594  6.900  6.480  4.520  7.402  10.134 7.752  8.328  9.554  120.89 1.00 .00 .00 1.00 5.888  1.00 .950
1.00   .00   .00   6.370  9.260  9.976  7.474  7.474  6.754  5.004  6.848  10.500 109.74 2.00 1.00 1.00 1.00 10.912 1.00 1.504
2.00  2.00  2.00   1.792  2.860  6.622  4.520  5.926  5.128  5.748  2.550  9.390  94.12  1.00 .00 .00 .00 5.204  .00 .721
 .00  1.00  1.00   8.356  6.800  6.326  6.396  5.940  7.958  4.334  10.016 10.278 123.40 1.00 1.00 1.00 1.00 8.946  .00 2.411
 .00  2.00  2.00   3.320  6.640  9.074  6.388  6.102  6.510  7.206  2.550  5.002  97.32  .00 .00 1.00 .00 4.432  1.00 .840
1.00  1.00   .00   7.672  10.580 5.748  6.760  3.866  6.760  7.964  6.782  80.35  2.00 .00 1.00 .00 7.774  1.00 -1.356
2.00  2.00  1.00   4.660  8.980  7.954  6.872  4.646  6.434  7.000  6.694  7.700  91.18  2.00 1.00 .00 .00 9.442  1.00 -.970
1.00  2.00   .00   5.048  7.560  9.174  9.762  7.430  8.610  2.804  8.740  6.798  110.89 .00 .00 1.00 .00 10.106 .00 -.330
1.00  1.00  1.00   7.724  5.560  6.610  5.546  5.794  6.544  6.658  6.134  7.482  94.12  1.00 1.00 1.00 .00 10.690 .00 -2.043
 .00   .00   .00   9.746  6.560  7.066  8.490  6.704  7.904  7.880  6.314  4.494  123.40 1.00 .00 .00 1.00 10.912 1.00 -.937
 .00  2.00  1.00   3.050  8.580  6.622  7.540  5.960  5.960  7.706  8.514  9.344  97.32  2.00 .00 .00 .00 5.204  1.00 -1.467
2.00  1.00  1.00   5.314  5.640  4.608  4.494  5.916  6.512  8.658  6.058  8.292  76.99  2.00 1.00 .00 .00 7.774  .00 -.313
1.00   .00  1.00   7.998  10.740 7.222  7.252  9.448  10.248 5.990  8.042  8.720  111.09 1.00 .00 .00 1.00 9.442  1.00 -.928
1.00  1.00   .00   7.704  3.040  7.352  4.678  6.506  8.854  6.802  10.490 8.710  108.85 2.00 1.00 1.00 1.00 6.190  .00 -.357
2.00  2.00  2.00   6.938  8.480  7.776  4.556  4.124  7.464  9.210  8.426  3.478  105.64 .00 .00 .00 .00 6.456  .00
1.00   .00  1.00   4.864  7.920  9.332  6.102  6.654  4.424  8.012  6.834  7.366  85.36  .00 .00 .00 .00 9.326  1.00
2.00  1.00  2.00   3.174  8.000  4.298  5.242  5.834  6.528  8.484  6.116  6.660  88.98  .00 1.00 1.00 1.00 5.580  1.00
1.00  1.00  1.00   7.198  2.960  1.524  1.524  5.834  6.332  8.062  5.978  10.516 120.76 .00 1.00 1.00 1.00 6.098  1.00
2.00  2.00  2.00   6.686  7.520  8.394  7.614  11.222 9.008  9.920  10.424 11.396 90.39  2.00 1.00 1.00 1.00 6.604  1.00
```

APPENDIX A: AIR TRAFFIC CONTROLLER DATA SET (Continued)

CONS	JOBPERF	FIELD	TRNGVID1	RACECAT	IQ1	NUM1SP1	NUM1SP2	NUM1SP3	NUM2SP1	NUM2SP2	NUM2SP3	NUM3SP1	NUM3SP2	NUM3SP3	TRICAF	DISPCAT1
-.288	7.618	.00	.00	2.00	110.47	7.032	9.162	9.248	8.744	7.888	5.530	5.522	7.880	6.264	1.00	1.00
.384	3.438	.00	.00	2.00	77.13	8.090	8.034	10.802	8.468	7.182	8.134	9.836	6.680	9.634	.00	.00
.129	11.600	1.00	1.00	1.00	91.27	12.028	10.892	10.396	8.210	7.756	7.562	10.100	6.220	7.732	1.00	1.00
-.259	5.838	1.00	1.00	2.00	68.28	9.872	10.080	4.158	6.764	9.558	6.066	7.996	8.380	5.904	.00	2.00
.210	10.078	.00	.00	.00	102.19	7.864	6.922	8.058	8.084	6.844	8.058	8.074	6.340	8.318	.00	.00
-.788	8.704	.00	1.00	1.00	96.93	6.688	9.692	7.226	6.288	6.084	7.392	7.324	7.100	5.494	.00	2.00
.104	6.034	1.00	1.00	1.00	90.24	10.150	7.832	10.082	5.778	4.812	3.442	8.040	6.360	5.870	.00	2.00
.917	7.484	.00	.00	.00	101.22	9.348	6.886	8.864	8.990	9.094	9.094	7.586	6.480	6.970	1.00	1.00
-.171	6.638	.00	1.00	.00	109.21	9.786	8.806	10.796	4.810	6.294	2.622	6.294	8.560	7.344	.00	1.00
-.109	8.196	.00	1.00	.00	118.96	8.006	3.998	6.244	9.494	4.884	3.818	9.392	4.260	5.422	2.00	1.00
.876	8.824	1.00	1.00	2.00	93.96	8.680	7.892	7.266	7.860	6.880	6.774	4.694	7.760	4.678	2.00	1.00
-1.038	9.500	.00	.00	2.00	143.79	10.334	7.274	6.068	5.292	6.978	6.196	6.934	5.380	2.370	.00	.00
-1.497	4.806	.00	1.00	2.00	82.59	9.800	8.220	5.756	7.332	4.206	7.332	3.998	6.600	7.096	1.00	1.00
-.336	6.254	1.00	.00	2.00	127.02	6.350	10.328	8.832	9.560	8.848	8.496	7.976	4.500	3.732	.00	.00
-1.465	9.720	1.00	1.00	1.00	100.62	7.140	5.694	4.930	7.076	9.158	7.012	10.946	7.400	6.516	2.00	1.00
1.957	10.050	1.00	.00	.00	106.99	7.458	5.984	2.512	7.854	7.904	4.554	4.184	6.640	3.662	1.00	.00
-.117	10.982	.00	.00	1.00	92.17	10.792	6.558	5.178	5.268	6.488	3.892	6.690	4.980	4.108	2.00	.00
.578	11.588	.00	1.00	.00	105.93	7.794	6.300	8.922	9.892	9.516	7.924	7.996	7.260	4.512	.00	1.00
3.613	7.838	1.00	.00	2.00	113.92	5.620	7.828	5.718	8.670	5.762	4.620	6.926	7.000	3.362	2.00	2.00
.609	9.816	1.00	1.00	2.00	103.95	6.122	8.466	6.956	6.360	6.062	4.254	5.090	5.860	5.092	1.00	.00
-1.275	5.768	1.00	.00	1.00	103.51	13.690	8.654	8.872	7.370	7.262	7.704	8.268	6.680	7.336	1.00	2.00
.153	9.878	1.00	1.00	2.00	99.34	11.906	10.986	7.794	8.770	6.382	9.970	8.616	4.780	4.430	1.00	2.00
-.261	8.710	1.00	1.00	1.00	99.63	6.880	6.744	8.818	6.266	7.728	6.131	5.974	6.580	6.586	2.00	2.00
.677	8.724	1.00	1.00	1.00	129.79	6.720	6.414	8.454	6.790	8.918	5.554	4.440	5.360	4.262	2.00	1.00
-.364	8.546	1.00	1.00	.00	93.33	5.840	5.070	6.996	3.570	6.076	7.170	5.766	8.220	7.992	2.00	.00
.676	7.896	1.00	1.00	2.00	134.49	7.066	8.290	7.200	9.810	7.902	6.694	5.174	6.660	2.280	2.00	2.00
-.434	5.912	1.00	1.00	1.00	100.69	7.222	6.236	5.062	5.988	6.834	5.274	3.122	3.640	7.966	.00	2.00
-.225	6.780	1.00	1.00	2.00	113.62	8.068	9.584	8.672	7.626	5.336	5.154	6.896	5.940	3.890	.00	2.00
-.551	5.832	.00	1.00	1.00	72.01	8.390	5.886	5.858	3.734	1.140	2.882	8.330	8.460	4.838	.00	2.00
-.651	9.620	1.00	1.00	1.00	82.51	8.816	6.802	5.924	8.554	1.928	3.300	5.994	5.440	4.542	2.00	1.00
-1.645	3.796	1.00	.00	2.00	69.64	9.474	8.452	11.586	6.360	7.956	8.406	4.804	8.040	8.340	.00	.00
-.398	7.580	.00	1.00	.00	116.49	9.858	8.872	7.816	10.018	2.714	7.466	7.338	2.520	2.984	1.00	2.00
-.159	11.742	.00	.00	.00	102.18	6.822	7.132	8.120	3.208	5.922	8.360	8.528	6.020	8.942	.00	.00
1.091	10.360	.00	1.00	1.00	119.82	4.400	1.058	1.572	6.854	2.892	2.892	3.460	2.800	2.984	.00	.00
-.420	8.536	1.00	.00	2.00	104.76	7.126	8.538	7.408	7.934	5.922	8.594	8.278	7.800	4.510	.00	.00
.665	7.614	1.00	.00	1.00	117.12	7.188	5.242	7.058	6.270	4.956	4.876	6.256	9.960	6.250	1.00	1.00
.754	9.490	.00	.00	.00	111.25	11.310	7.574	10.716		8.332	5.982	6.802	9.580	7.458	1.00	1.00

CONS = conscientiousness; JOBPERF = task performance; FIELD = field independence; TRNGVID1 = training video; RACECAT = race category; IQ1 = intelligence; NUM1SP1–NUM3SP3 = task performance in each of the nine possible combinations of the target number and target speed variables; TRICAF = amount of caffeine; DISPCAT1 = display category.

APPENDIX B: DERIVATION FOR EQUATION (4.7)

Y' is used to indicate the dependent variable in question with the two covariates X_1 and X_2 covaried out. Then

$$\text{VAR } Y' = \text{VAR}\{Y - [b_1(X_1 - X_1) + b_2(X_2 - X_2)]\}$$

$$= s_Y^2 + \text{VAR}[b_1(X_1 - X_1) + b_2(X_2 - X_2)]$$

$$- 2\text{COV}\{Y, [b_1(X_1 - X_1) + b_2(X_2 - X_2)]\}$$

$$= s_Y^2 + b_1^2 s_{X1}^2 + b_2^2 s_{X2}^2 + 2b_1 b_2 \text{COV}(X_1, X_2)$$

$$- 2b_1 \text{COV}(X_1, Y) - 2b_2 \text{COV}(X_2, Y).$$

Equation (4.7) calls for the square root of this value

$$\{s_Y^2 + b_1^2 s_{X1}^2 + b_2^2 s_{X2}^2 + 2b_1 b_2 \text{COV}(X_1, X_2)$$

$$- 2b_1 \text{COV}(X_1, Y) - 2b_2 \text{COV}(X_2, Y)\}^{.5}.$$

REFERENCES

ARVEY, R. D., & COLE, D. A. (1989) Evaluating change due to training. In I. L. Goldstein & Assoc. (Eds.), *Training and development in organizations*. San Francisco, CA: Jossey-Bass.

ARVEY, R. D., COLE, D. A., HAZUCHA, J., & HARTANTO, F. (1985) Statistical power of training evaluation designs. *Personnel Psychology*, *38*, 493–507.

BECKER, B. J. (1988) Synthesizing standardized mean change measures. *British Journal of Mathematical and Statistical Psychology*, *41*, 257–278.

COHEN, J. (1969) *Statistical power analysis for the behavioral sciences*. Orlando, FL: Academic Press.

COHEN, J. (1977) *Statistical power analysis for the behavioral sciences* (2nd ed.). Orlando, FL: Academic Press.

CORTINA, J. M., & DESHON, R. P. (1998) Determining relative importance of predictors with the observational design. *Journal of Applied Psychology*, *83*, 798–804.

CORTINA, J. M., & DUNLAP, W. P. (1997) On the logic and purpose of significance testing. *Psychological Methods*, *2*, 161–172.

DUNLAP, W. P., CORTINA, J. M., VASLOW, J. B., & BURKE, M. J. (1996) Meta-analysis of experiments with matched groups or repeated measures designs. *Psychological Methods*, *1*, 170–177.

GLASS, G. V., MCGAW, B., & SMITH, M. L. (1981) *Meta-analysis in social research*. Newbury Park, CA: Sage.

HEDGES, L. V. (1981) Distribution theory for Glass' estimator of effect size and related estimators. *Journal of Educational Statistics*, *6*, 107–128.

HEDGES, L. V., & OLKIN, I. (1985) *Statistical methods for meta-analysis*. Orlando, FL: Academic Press.

HUNTER, J. E., & SCHMIDT, F. L. (1990) *Methods of meta-analysis: Correcting error and bias in research findings*. Newbury Park, CA: Sage.

JORESKOG, K., & SORBOM, D. (1996) *PRELIS 2: User's Reference Guide*. Chicago, IL: SSI, Inc.

MEEHL, P. E. (1990). Why summaries of research on psychological theories are often uninterpretable. [Monograph Suppl. 1-V66]. *Psychological Reports*, *66*, 195–244.

MORRIS, S. B., & DESHON, R. P. (1997) Correcting effect sizes computed from factorial analysis of variance for use in meta-analysis. *Psychological Methods*, *2*, 192–199.

NOURI, H., & GREENBERG, R. H. (1995). Meta-analytic procedures for estimation of effect sizes in experiments using complex analysis of variance. *Journal of Management*, *21*, 801–812.

RAY, J. W., & SHADISH, W. (1996) How interchangeable are different estimators of effect size? *Journal of Consulting and Clinical Psychology*, *64*, 1316–1325.

ROSENTHAL, R. (1991) *Meta-analytic Procedures for Social Research*. Newbury Park, CA: Sage.

ABOUT THE AUTHORS

JOSE M. CORTINA is an Associate Professor of Industrial/Organizational Psychology at George Mason University. He received his Ph.D. from Michigan State University in 1994 under the tutelage of Neal Schmitt. He teaches, conducts research, and consults in a wide variety of statistical and methodological areas as well as areas relating to personnel selection and human resource management. His work has appeared in *Journal of Applied Psychology, Psychological Methods, Personnel Psychology, Applied Psychological Measurement,* and *Journal of Management* among others. He is of the opinion that the QASS series is pretty much the best thing since sliced bread, and he is pleased to be a part of it.

HOSSEIN NOURI is a Professor of Accountancy in the School of Business at The College of New Jersey. He earned his Ph.D. degree in accounting from Temple University in 1992. His research interests are in areas of meta-analysis and behavioral accounting. His articles on such topics as meta-analysis, participative budgeting, and budgetary slack have appeared in the *Journal of Management, Accounting, Organizations, and Society, Behavioral Research in Accounting,* and *Journal of Accounting Literature.* Before joining academia, he worked as an audit manager for public accounting firms. He is also a Certified Public Accountant, Certified Fraud Examiner, and Certified Financial Services Auditor.

ACKNOWLEDGMENTS

Our many thanks to Adam Winsler, David Costanza, Kim Eby, Rick DeShon, Michael Lewis-Beck, and one anonymous reviewer for their invaluable comments on portions of this manuscript.

Correspondence regarding this monograph should be sent to Jose Cortina, Department of Psychology, George Mason University, Fairfax, VA 22030.